# Independent School Entrance

## Victoria Barker

Edited by Emma Bartley

Published by
Gresham Books Limited
The Carriage House
Ningwood Manor
Ningwood
Isle of Wight
PO30 4NJ

Main Cover Image: Handcross Park School, handcrossparkschool.co.uk

ISBN 978-0-946095-59-9

Design by Words & Pictures
Typesetting and layout by Fiona Jerome
Printed by Cambrian Printers

# Independent School Entrance

## Victoria Barker

# Independent School Entrance

# CONTENTS

Above left:
Canford School

Above:
Bethany School

Far left:
Hawkesdown
House Prep.
Photo: Eaton &
Woods

Left: Finton
House Prep

Below: Royal
Grammar School,
Guildford

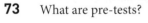

# Introduction

Like anything else in life, choosing an independent school for your child is far less daunting if the process is demystified. One of the problems about independent schools—in the past at least—is that they have been shrouded in myth and stereotype, and parents are not getting the facts they need. It's timely then that parents should have access to a practical, no-nonsense guide such as this, packed with useful information. Anyone contemplating a 21st century independent education for their child cannot help but reach for it with a sigh of relief.

And as it's the 21st century, a word first about the dangers of overthinking the whole thing and, yes, about stress. There is lots in this book about how to reassure your child, both during the entrance exam process and also when starting school. In my experience, however, it's often the parents who develop sweaty palms and a slight stomach ache on the day. My friendly advice is to turn off your iPhone, do your homework and prepare your child, but keep your own anxieties under control. If you are committed to choosing the right independent school and then placing your child in its care, you need to be calm. So take a deep breath, read the manual and then trust the process.

The strengths of the modern independent sector are fully explored in the pages that follow and it's a powerful picture. For the essence of what makes these schools great, I'd go no further than the name: 'independent'. Thanks to long tradition, excellent resources, committed and imaginative teaching and an aspirational ethos, independent schools have character, individuality and breadth of vision. In being less constrained in what they offer, they can cater for specialist interests such as music, drama and sport, or special needs such as enrichment work or learning support. They are likely to have a wide co-curricular programme, with clubs and societies and many other activities complementing the academic programme. Most of all, however, they have the staff to tailor education to the needs of each child. That way, all pupils feel valued and grow up in a vibrant environment for learning.

Those pupils now come from all kinds of families, and fee-paying education is no longer the preserve of the few. Fresh air and a spirit of social change is blowing through independent schools, and it is high time. There's plenty of advice here about applying for bursaries; payment schemes are much more agile than they were, reflecting a new awareness of the very significant commitment that school

fees represent. Families with a broad range of incomes can now benefit from part or full bursaries, and schools work carefully with each family to get that level right. A student who left my school recently, having received a seven-year full bursary, said that it had been the most incredible and life-changing gift she had ever received. She certainly enriched the school as a highly talented and exceptional young woman and her words made me reflect anew about the lifelong gift that a great education represents. There really is nothing more important, or lasting, that any of us could provide for our children. I hope that in reading this book you will come to know even more clearly what independent schools have to offer, and feel encouraged as you travel the road towards finding the right school for your own son or daughter.

Clarissa Farr
High Mistress,
St Paul's Girls' School

# About the Author

Victoria Barker is a parent with one child in a London girls' school and another who has recently completed A levels. She has taught in both secondary and tertiary sectors, and has written a number of children's educational resources. Victoria is also the author of *The 11+ and 13+ Handbook: A Parent's Guide to the Selection Process for Independent Schools in the UK*, and runs the Independent Junction website, which provides

resources for parents in the independent sector. Victoria was inspired to write for The Parent Brief because of her experience arriving in the UK from Australia and discovering how hard it was to make sense of the school system. On asking her British friends, she found that they were having the same problem. After eight years in this country she has certainly mastered the UK education system—if not the accent!

# HOW DOES THE INDEPENDENT SYSTEM WORK?

If you are new to schooling in the UK, at whatever level, you will probably feel at the bottom of a very steep learning curve.

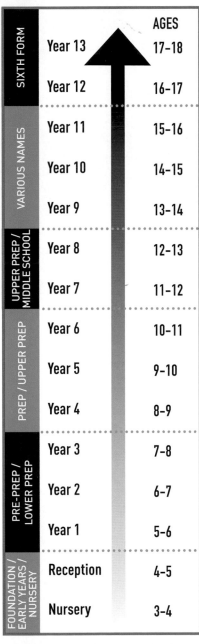

| | | AGES |
|---|---|---|
| SIXTH FORM | Year 13 | 17–18 |
| | Year 12 | 16–17 |
| VARIOUS NAMES | Year 11 | 15–16 |
| | Year 10 | 14–15 |
| | Year 9 | 13–14 |
| UPPER PREP / MIDDLE SCHOOL | Year 8 | 12–13 |
| | Year 7 | 11–12 |
| PREP / UPPER PREP | Year 6 | 10–11 |
| | Year 5 | 9–10 |
| | Year 4 | 8–9 |
| PRE-PREP / LOWER PREP | Year 3 | 7–8 |
| | Year 2 | 6–7 |
| | Year 1 | 5–6 |
| FOUNDATION / EARLY YEARS / NURSERY | Reception | 4–5 |
| | Nursery | 3–4 |

This table reflects the English system. Rest of the UK varies

Finton House
Pre-Prep and
Prep School

The naming conventions of independent schools differ from state schools and also, often, from each other's. Some schools have their own, highly idiosyncratic naming conventions. At the senior level, 'Fourth Form' may refer to entirely different years at different schools.

- Ages 3–4: these years may be called Nursery, Foundation or Early Years.
- Ages 4–7: these years are usually called Pre-Prep (though in the all-through schools, this may be Lower Prep).
- Ages 7–11: these years are usually called Prep (in the all-through schools, this may be Upper Prep).
- Ages 11–13: these years are usually called Upper Prep (in the all-through schools, this may be Middle School).
- Ages 13–16: the names for these years depend on whether the school starts at Year 9 or is an all-through school, or only continues to Year 11: it may be Lower School, Middle School or Upper School—or another name entirely.
- Ages 16–18: this is usually (though not universally) called Sixth Form: Lower Sixth and Upper Sixth.

Independent schools do not need to follow the National Curriculum, but it is helpful to know the terminology.

In England, Wales and Northern Ireland, there are five Key Stages (KS):

- KS1: Years 1 and 2, for children aged 5–7;
- KS2: Years 3–6, for children aged 7–11;
- KS3: Years 7–9, for children aged 11–14;
- KS4: Years 10 and 11, for children aged 14–16, leading to GCSE or its equivalent;
- KS5: Years 12 and 13, for 16+, covering Sixth Form qualifications.

Students at
King's School,
Canterbury

# WHY
## SHOULD WE CONSIDER AN
# INDEPENDENT SCHOOL?

**The achievements of independent schools in the UK are hard to dispute, but this is just one reason to consider an independent education for your child.**

In general, many parents choose independent schools for their children because of the excellent qualifications and ambitious university applications associated with these schools: students from independent schools are more likely to win places at the best universities in the UK and abroad, particularly at Oxbridge and Russell Group universities. (You may hear in the media that universities discriminate against independent school children; this is simply not true. While they do seek to give opportunities to less privileged children, they are most interested in what a pupil is capable of achieving—which is demonstrated best by prior performance.)

Independent schools generally offer better facilities: large grounds, arts centres, theatres and so on. Independent schools also have better teacher:pupil ratios, often better than 1:10. Smaller classes represent more individualised teaching. Children are encouraged to approach teachers outside class about their work; it is common for children in independent schools to form strong bonds with their teachers.

### Extra-curricular activity

Independent school children are well represented at the highest levels in competitive sport. Schools offer a wide range of extra-curricular activities: sports, music, drama and dance; bookbinding, beekeeping, taekwondo, glass-blowing and silversmithing. Students go off to amazing places to do amazing things: to Darwin to race in the World Solar Challenge, to Florida to compete in the NASA Space Challenge, to the Vatican to sing, to Everest to

raise money for local orphanages, to the Arctic to complete their Duke of Edinburgh Awards. A number of schools send productions to the Edinburgh Festival; others have members of the National Youth Choir and National Youth Orchestra; many schools have pupils who play in national sport teams. The schools

> **Independent schools generally achieve higher grades than non-selective state schools: pupils are more likely to attain A/A\* grades at GCSE and A levels. Furthermore, these marks are earned in the more difficult subjects, such as modern languages and hard sciences.**
>
> Taken from the Independent Schools Council website

> More than half of pupils at schools in the Independent Schools Council achieve A/A\* grades at A levels, compared to a national average of 27%.
>
> Figures from the Independent Schools Council

attract illustrious speakers: parliamentarians, CEOs, the heads of charities, NGOs and major political organisations. Some have sports teachers who are Olympic champions.

## Individuality

Independent schools have greater flexibility in their hiring of staff: they can take strong teachers directly from Russell Group universities, without requiring a postgraduate teaching qualification. Their teachers are subject specialists—many with Masters or PhDs—and there is an assumption that these teachers will communicate their passion to their pupils. Independent schools also have greater flexibility in the curriculum and the awards they offer: many schools offer IGCSE

> 38% of UK medal winners in the 2012 Olympics came from ISC schools, which accounts for just 7% of schoolchildren.

Cranleigh Prep horse rider

and Cambridge pre-U courses, which are held to be more rigorous.

## Term times

Independent school hours are usually longer than those of state schools, and Saturday morning may be part of the school week. Because of this, term times are shorter.

## Ethos

Perhaps the most substantial difference between independent schools and state-funded schools is ethos. Independent schools educate the 'whole child'. While academic attainment is valued highly, it is not as a rule considered the sole, or sometimes even the most important, value. Priority is given to skills that help children flourish more widely: open-mindedness, leadership and compassion.

## Tradition

Along with a forward-thinking outlook, these schools have strong traditions. The prestige of some independent schools derives from their history: in some, the alumni are pivotal historical figures in various fields. (20 British prime ministers were educated at Eton alone.)

## Internationalism

Today's independent schools are thoroughly global, with a larger international cohort than state-funded schools. School prospectuses commonly highlight the fact that 40 or more nationalities are represented. This mix of outlooks contributes to a broader understanding and global perspective that is of enormous value to pupils, who emerge from these schools with networks of friends from around the world. These are young people who expect to live their lives on a global stage. ■

Downside School bagpipe player

### STRAIGHT FROM THE HORSE'S MOUTH

"Independent schools give children a respect for excellence, teamwork, humour and debate which is dynamic, intelligent, irreverent and polite, all at the same time. This educational environment allows pupils to question authority, but insists on civilised rules of engagement while doing so. Pupils thrive through the sheer range of experiences on offer. These schools respect and acknowledge skills not quantifiable in a teacher's mark book or a league table. Independent schools have what I call the 'and' culture: it is not football or maths; it's football and maths; it's tennis and dancing; trumpet and coding; acting and physics. My school, at least, provides a world-class, timeless education unfettered by ephemeral governmental politics. Finally, independent schools tend to have a great atmosphere of fun."

**TOM ROGERSON, HEADMASTER OF COTTESMORE**

### HOW I FOUND...

## MY INDEPENDENT SCHOOL EDUCATION

"I've no doubt that I benefitted from an independent education. There's an ethos in independent schools that you should always try your hardest. This may come primarily from the home environment, but it is promoted by all those children working in close proximity with the same ethos driving them. I'm a teacher in a state school now, and this ethos seems to be missing from many of the schools I've experienced."

**Sophie, former boarder in a country boarding school**

# WHAT WILL AN INDEPENDENT SCHOOL EDUCATION ACTUALLY COST?

**The cost of an independent school education can add up to substantially more than the school fees.**

Information on costs is available on schools' websites or in the pack given out to prospective parents. Consider: is this cost sustainable for all of your child's school years? What will you have to sacrifice to pay the fees, with what effect on your family life? Can you afford the fees for the siblings who follow?

The costs of an independent education vary considerably. There may not be a huge difference between London and the rest of England, though Scotland, Ireland and Wales are often less expensive. It depends more on the type of school. The most expensive are the famous boarding schools; the least expensive are small country day schools. Boarding schools tend to charge more, even for day pupils, because their extensive provision is available to all. Some schools charge more for incoming Sixth Form students; some give a sibling discount, though this may not be much.

## School trips

Some trips are both compulsory and charged, such as for pupils studying a language at GCSE or A levels. Geography, History and Classical Civilisation students may also go abroad. If your child plays a team sport, there may be matches nationally or even internationally. The same may apply to debating or other clubs. Some trips are optional—until all your child's friends are going. Some schools try to keep costs down, others book luxury hotels. Some try to warn parents in advance of costs; others may simply add them to the bill.

## When will I have to pay?

Fees are usually due on the first day of term, but can often be paid in instalments. Some schools discount fees paid ahead for the child's entire education. A term's notice of intention to withdraw is required, or a term's fees will be forfeited. If parents fall behind, some schools will try to accommodate and may offer bursaries in case of crisis; others charge late fees and/or exclude the child after a warning. ∎

> **The less expensive schools include:** some of the former grammar schools, some of which have retained 'Grammar' in their name; the schools associated with livery companies, which may have old-fashioned words like 'haberdashers' and 'mercers' in their names; and some of the schools of the Girls' Day School Trust (GDST).

> **HERE TO HELP**
>
> "It's worth noting that 'extras' can add considerably to the bill (as much as another 10%) depending on the activities your child chooses to take part in, such as music tuition or school trips. Allowance should be made for expenses related to books, entries for public examinations, stationery and uniforms." **MARK TAYLOR,** BURSAR AT KING'S SCHOOL, CANTERBURY

Dulwich College, where places are highly sought after, and around 25% of boys receive Bursary or Scholarship assistance

# 10 **EXTRA COSTS** YOU MAY FACE

**1** **Registration fees** are around £100–£200. Common Entrance exams may cost £300–£500. On accepting a place, a deposit is due: either as a flat fee (£800–£3000) or around half the termly fee. A portion may be subtracted from the first and/or final bill. Overseas parents may be charged a larger deposit.

**2** Fees may or may not include **textbooks and stationery**, which may be added to the bill.

**3** Fees may or may not include **school lunches**, usually charged at roughly £200 per term.

**4** Fees will not include **uniforms**. These vary in price, with a full outfit (including sports kit) potentially setting you back up to £500 or more.

**5** Schools typically charge £200–£300 per term for 30-minute **music classes**; more for longer sessions. Some schools offer small group classes less expensively.

**6** Particularly in boarding schools, all options may be included in the fee. Others charge for **extra-curriculars**: drama, sports training, counselling or ESL. Some charge for rowing, sailing, riding, tennis or fencing.

**7** There will be a charge for participating in the **Combined Cadet Force** and the **Duke of Edinburgh Awards**. Participation is normally optional.

**8** **Entering exams** costs £30–£40 per subject at GCSE, more for modern languages, and more again for A level subjects.

**9** Fees may be charged for '**late stays**' after normal school hours.

**10** **School trips** are a further—and significant—expense.

**Fees are per term, three terms a year.**

• **Pre-prep schools:** Fees for full-time nursery and pre-preps vary, from under £2000 per term to over £3000.

• **Prep schools:** Some prestigious London preps are well over £6000 per term; country preps are often £4000–£5000. Full boarding is typically £6500–£7500 but may be much higher. Very few full-boarding preps charge less than £6000 per term.

• **Senior day schools:** Standard fees are £4000–£6000 per term, though you will find outliers at either end. Day school fees at boarding schools are not much different from boarding fees, and may be up to £8000–£9000 per term.

• **Full boarding senior schools:** Elite schools typically charge £11,000–£12,000 per term for full boarding; a few are now over £12,000 and more will follow. However, many charge £8000–£10,000; only a handful charge less than £8000.

# IS FINANCIAL HELP AVAILABLE?

**If an independent school education seems unattainable due to the expense, you may like to know that there are lots of options for financial support.**

A young musician at Handcross Park School

## SHOULD I ENQUIRE ABOUT A BURSARY?

The message of independent school Heads is clear: do not hesitate to say that you need financial help. Heads are keenly aware that their schools are expensive—prohibitively so for many families. There is no need to feel embarrassed about admitting financial need in the face of so huge a commitment.

Financial aid is part of the remit of the schools; it is part of the job of those to whom you will speak when applying. Most schools have bursary funds, some of which date back hundreds of years. Bursars actively try to find recipients for these funds. Matching bursaries to families is not a matter of charity, but simply part of the

school's work—and the work of its Bursar. Most independent schools strive to do all they can to accommodate children from less privileged backgrounds.

Everyone understands that asking for financial help is not easy. These Heads point out that the Registrars and Bursars are so accustomed to questions about financial support and requests from those seeking financial support that there is nothing you can ask that has not been asked many times before.

One last point: the awarding of bursaries is strictly confidential. The members of the school community are not likely to know which children are bursary recipients.

The Independent Schools Council reports that over one third of students in its member schools are receiving help with fees of one kind or another. Assistance may come from the schools themselves, from the schools' charitable foundations, or from one of the charitable trusts established in the UK to target children's welfare. The ISC also points out that this number is growing, year on year, as the schools work harder to top up their bursary funds by seeking sponsorships or by diverting funds from other projects.

Many schools have appropriated scholarship monies for their bursary funds, so that financial assistance may be directed to families in the greatest need. Some independent schools are dispersing millions of pounds a year from these bursary funds and offering dozens of places with up to 100% fee remission. Some of this country's most prestigious schools have a stated objective

Performers from Bedales

of becoming 'needs blind' within the next generation.

## Applying for a bursary

Each school or charitable institution will disburse its funds using its own systems and criteria. You should make an effort to establish the criteria used by the different schools and institutions. General information can be found on school websites, but information specific to your circumstances must be obtained from the Registrars and Bursars.

Schools do not generally give an indication of the income of successful bursary applicants. As a rough guide, if you are applying for a bursary at one of the London schools, and your combined family income is less than £20,000 or so, a bursary may cover the full fees; if your combined income is over £45,000–£50,000, you are unlikely to qualify. At some schools, the threshold may be up to £60,000–70,000, but this is unusual. Outside cities, thresholds are normally lower.

It will take some effort to document your application. Be aware that a school will look at your financial position very closely: your income, your mortgage, the cars you drive, the holidays you take, jewellery, art, antiques and so on. Some people find this intrusive, but schools want to know that bursaries go to those whose need is greatest. Bursary funds are not limitless, so you will be competing against others. A small family who owns a large family house will be judged less needy than another family who rent a small apartment. Similarly, if you are a two-parent family with only one parent working, the school may wish to know your plans for the other parent to find work. Bear in mind that many families drive their finances into the ground to afford independent

school fees, and it is certainly not unknown for family homes to be sold or remortgaged. If only in fairness to such families, a Bursar will want to know that your need is genuine. The Admissions staff may visit your home to ensure that your situation is as you have represented it.

Bear in mind also that the cost of going to an independent school is not limited to the fees themselves. There will also be charges for uniforms, trips, music equipment, music lessons, sports equipment, sports tours, books, laptops, stationery, exams and so on. As a rule

of thumb, at least a further 10% is needed on top of the school fees to allow for these extra expenses. These expenses will be patchy: some school terms will be more expensive than others. These extra expenses should be factored into your bursary application.

The question of finances is not, however, the most important thing in determining whether a bursary application will be successful. The most important thing will be your child. First of all, schools consider applicants independent of finances and whether they fit the school profile. Only once ▶

Holmewood House School's Scholars

**THESE MAY HELP**

Chorister places are generally subsidised to begin with, and the Choir School Scholarship Scheme (choirschools.org.uk) provides further means-tested funds. The Music and Dance scheme (gov.uk/music-dance-scheme) offers means-tested support and grants for musicians and dancers.

The Charities Commission (found through gov.uk) keeps details of all charities providing specialised bursaries, and the Educational Trusts Forum (educational-grants.org) details those for families who cannot afford fees.

The Good Schools Guide Advice Service will be able to give you personalised advice that fits your specific needs.

the school is convinced that a child will benefit by joining the school community—and vice versa—will it consider your eligibility for a bursary. Thus the school will focus on your child's academic ability or other skills. Follow the school's lead: this is what you should focus on if you wish to gain a bursary. Your aim is to make your child appear as attractive as possible to a prospective school.

Your child will stand a greater chance of gaining a bursary if they have proven achievements. Many schools award scholarships on the basis of academic, sporting and artistic ability, and give bursaries to scholarship recipients before others. For these schools, the aim of gaining a bursary is thus secondary to the prior aim of gaining a scholarship, since the bursary is in effect a paid scholarship. **(For more on scholarships, see p. 63, or p. 106 for Sixth Form.)**

Even where schools do not prioritise scholarship winners, evidence that a child will help the school's exam results or make a specific contribution to a school's orchestra or football team will not be overlooked. A previous connection to the school will sometimes help a bursary application.

Be aware that most bursaries are reassessed annually. If your financial circumstances improve, your bursary may be withdrawn. Equally, if you already have a school place and your circumstances change for the worse, you may be able to secure a bursary ahead of others.

## Available bursaries

The best place to go for information is to the schools themselves. The Bursars and Admission Staff will explain how bursaries are administered and advise whether you fit the criteria. They may also know about other sources of funding and may even approach funding bodies with your child in mind.

Many of the schools with large charitable foundations are very old. Some of these foundations go back to medieval times. (If you read about a 'Queen's Scholarship' fund set up by Queen Elizabeth, for example, do not assume that the present queen is responsible.) At that time, these 'public' schools were for boys only. As a result, total bursary funds allocated across the UK may skew towards male recipients. Be this as it may, there are a large number of scholarships at the old public

schools that provide a path not only to the school itself, but also to a bursary.

If your child has skills in the creative arts—in music, voice or dance—there may be funded places at specialised independent schools. Other scholarships are more specific again: if a member of your family belongs to a certain profession, there may be bursaries from the livery company associated with that profession. There are specific bursaries for the children of clergy and seafarers, those who have worked in the City of London and, at Sixth Form, to future members of the armed services.

## If your bursary application is unsuccessful

Think about what you want to do if you are not awarded a bursary at a school for which your child is applying. Some schools, it appears, tend not to offer places at all to bursary applicants whose bursary application is unsuccessful. You are therefore strongly advised to inform the school if you wish to be considered for a place for your child, even if you are not successful in gaining a bursary. This of course raises a difficulty: the school will wish to know how you plan to pay the fees in the absence of a bursary. Perhaps you might explain that you would consider remortgaging your house (for example) if a bursary were not available, but that you would only consider this option as a last resort. ∎

**HERE TO HELP**

"Research carefully and do explore the schools' websites, but above all, do not be afraid to ask the schools exactly what they have on offer."

**MARK TAYLOR, BURSAR AT KING'S SCHOOL, CANTERBURY**

Science at Cranleigh Senior School

**AUTHOR'S TIPS**

# 10 TIPS FOR BURSARY APPLICANTS

**1** There is no abstract metric used by schools to assess who is awarded a bursary; each application is considered on its own merits. **Make it clear from the outset** that you are thinking of applying for a bursary, so as to get the best advice from the school at an early stage.

**2** Each school or institution has its own criteria for the award of bursaries. **It is not worth trying to fit yourself into a category where you do not fit**. Spend your time on applications with some prospect of success.

**3** The school **may consider the situation of your family as a whole**. So, for example, if a child has a brother or sister with special needs, the offer of a boarding school place may benefit both children, in that it frees the parents to care for the other child.

**4** Bursaries covering only a percentage of the school fees are generally more common than full-fee bursaries. You may stand a better chance of receiving a bursary if you can **contribute some percentage of the fees yourself**.

**5** Before accepting a bursary, **establish its duration**: you need to know that the level of the bursary will remain stable throughout your child's school career.

**6** It is best to **get started early** in your search for schools. Some children receive a bursary from prep school onwards and such a child may earn the support of the prep school Head in an application for a bursary at a senior school, which can be a great advantage.

**7** Those families seeking a bursary should avoid choosing a school based merely on the best offer financially. **The primary consideration should be whether the child is suited to the school**, rather than the value of the offer itself. It may be better to accept a smaller offer from a school where you are confident that your child will be both happy and academically successful.

**8** The award of a bursary will be subject to your child's success at the school. A bursary may be withdrawn if the recipient's behaviour or work is unsatisfactory. **Make sure your child is prepared to work hard** at their new school.

**9** Remember to **ask whether the school waives the registration fee** for bursary applicants.

**10** Note that bursaries are usually reserved for British citizens. If your legal status changes while your child is attending the school, they may then look upon a bursary request more favourably. If you have several children to put through school, and you are set on a British education for them, consider applying for British nationality well in advance of their starting school.

# HOW DO I APPLY FROM THE STATE SECTOR?

While many primary schools are used to sending children to the independent sector, some have little to no experience in this area.

For children at state primaries, gaining admission to a selective independent school can sometimes mean venturing into the unknown: no-one they know has any experience of it. If your child is coming from such a school, you may need to put more effort into the admissions process than other families who are already in the independent sector. You may need to do more careful research and rely more heavily on your own judgement than others who have the advantage of a prep school Head to advise them.

A state primary school in the UK is not designed to educate a child to the level required to excel in the exams set by selective independent schools for entry at 11+. The state sector has aimed to achieve a solid Level 4 or above for every child in the Year 6 National Curriculum tests (or SATs), whereas independent schools typically set their 11+ exams at Level 5—and they are often at the difficult end of this level. (These levels have been renamed 'bands' and their assessment has now changed slightly, but it is still true.)

You do not need to be familiar with this grading system. The point is merely that the level of achievement expected by many of the independent schools of children at age 11 is higher—and sometimes far higher—than is generally expected in state primaries. Even if your child is clever, they may still need to work independently to ▶

"Brace yourself for the selection process. When we made the switch, we assumed that because we were paying, we would have a choice—but this wasn't the case. The school will select the children they want to admit, so you need to make sure you are approaching the right kind of school for your child, where their talents will be recognised."

**CAMILLA, WHOSE CHILDREN TRANSFERRED TO A PREP SCHOOL IN YEAR 2**

## AUTHOR'S TIPS

# HOW SHOULD I APPROACH THE TOPIC WITH MY CHILD'S CURRENT STATE SCHOOL?

One difficulty that parents sometimes face is that state school teachers and Heads sometimes have an antipathy (however slight) towards the independent school sector in general. They may, for example, be peeved about the extra work involved in writing references for your child—work not required for pupils remaining within the state sector.

Any such antipathy will only be exacerbated by the questions that may appear on these forms. Independent schools may ask about a child's academic rank compared to others in their class, which will be off-putting to teachers whose overriding objective is to get every child to a reasonable level. Worse still are questions about whether your child's home life is 'conducive to success' at school. Many primary school teachers will be reluctant to answer questions such as these, on the grounds that they patently discriminate against children who, through no fault of their own, have a 'non-conducive' home life.

Try to ensure from the start that your present school will support your application, and that both Head and form teacher are prepared to write positive references for your child. If you are applying to a school where entry is highly competitive, you should inform both teacher and Head that your child may not succeed in gaining entry without their support. Don't assume that they will be fully aware of this.

Remember that the success of a prep school is judged partly on the destinations of its leavers, and so prep school Heads have an interest in writing glowing references. There is no such advantage to state school staff in writing these references. You might give some thought therefore to what you can do for your primary school, by way of reciprocity: helping children with reading, with school clubs and so on. Some state primaries have even started charging parents for these references: the going rate appears to be £50 per reference.

If your primary school appears less than fully supportive, you may wish to warn the senior school Registrar that the reference they receive for your child may not be as effusive as it might be. The Registrar will be aware that state school teachers and Heads have no great interest in these forms. Likewise, if you doubt that a reference will be sent from your primary to the senior school, you can always check with the Registrar at the appropriate time whether it has arrived. You might offer as a substitute your child's most recent school reports, which will provide some of the information the school wants. The school will simply have to rely more heavily on the other information that they have available to them: the exam results and interviews.

RIMDREAM/ISTOCK/THINKSTOCK

# 5 TIPS FOR STATE SCHOOL APPLICANTS

**1** Prep schools prepare pupils with exams frequently and rigorously. The only way to compensate for this lack of experience is to **set your child specimen exam papers** in exam-like conditions, strictly observed.

**2** If there are no others from your school moving to the independent sector, you will have to **rely heavily on your own initiative** throughout the admissions process. Be particularly careful with your research, because any misunderstandings will not be picked up in discussions at the school gate.

**3** **Do not be put off** applying to an independent school on the basis that your child will be unlike the other children in the school. Most independent schools have children of diverse backgrounds, nationalities, levels of privilege, abilities, interests and so on. If your child is successful at their school, other issues will be of secondary importance. Likewise, do not be put off applying to an independent school by any antipathy towards the independent sector others may express. Others are welcome to their opinions; nothing compels you to share them.

**4** Ensure that your chosen schools have a good attitude to children from the state sector. **Ask your guide** on the school tour: 'How many of the children at this school went to a state primary school?' If they don't know the answer, this is a good sign. Once a child has joined the school community, it should no longer be an issue what type of school they came from. The Admissions staff will nevertheless be able to tell you how many children come from state schools.

**5** **Do not feel too disadvantaged.** Some 'prep' schools provide surprisingly little preparation; if you and your child are willing to work hard, you stand every chance of getting in.

reach this higher level. For this reason, some parents decide to make the transition from the state to the independent sector

> "Get together with existing parents and the PTA. They will have good tips for you, and they may have old uniforms to pass or sell on."
> **SUSAN,** WHOSE DAUGHTER TRANSFERRED FROM THE STATE SECTOR IN YEAR 7

earlier, in Year 5 or 6, so that they have the advantage of applying to a senior school from within the independent sector. That's the bad news.

The good news is that, although it may be more difficult to enter an independent school from a state school, the difficulty is not too great. There is much more movement between the state and independent sectors than there was 10 or 20 years ago. An application from a state school will be nothing new to any independent school Registrar in the UK.

Some of London's top independents take more than half their cohort from the state sector at 11+.

More good news: while you do need to put effort into the admissions process, you do not need to go to the expense of hiring an advisor. Any information an advisor could give you can be obtained from the school's website, its ISI report and from a school visit. If you have specific questions, you can talk to school Admissions staff or, if you are truly stumped, you can visit an online forum and ask for advice there.

## Should we hire a tutor?

Some parents figure that the money they have saved on school fees during primary school can more profitably be spent on hiring a tutor at this stage. By all means, employ a tutor if you can afford it. However, it is expensive and involves work that, in many cases, can be done by a committed parent. Even if you employ a tutor several times a week, your own involvement will always be more important than the contribution a tutor can make, no matter how good. If you have a reasonable level of English and some basic skills in Maths, you can easily find out what needs to be done to help, obtain the materials and work through them with your child at home. You do not even need to buy preparation materials as there are a great number of practice papers and specimen exams available free online for you to download and use.

Independent schools tend to select children with a home life that is 'conducive to success', and the involvement of parents in the admissions process is evidence of this. Children may be asked at interview whether there is someone at home who helps them with their homework, exam preparation and so on. You want your child to be able to answer 'Yes!' to this question with some enthusiasm.

**(For more on tutors, see p. 70.)** ■

(For more on tutors, see p. 70.)

### THIS MAY HELP

You can find the links to over 200 free specimen exams on the Independent Junction website.

# WHAT DO I NEED TO KNOW ABOUT APPLYING
# FROM OVERSEAS?

**Increasingly, students are coming from across the globe to the UK to be educated in some of the best schools in the world.**

Senior boys at Halliford

For international students, there are many advantages to attending an independent school in the UK. They receive an exceptional level of education which will qualify them for university entrance anywhere in the world. Those coming to the country boarding schools will enjoy the idyllic environment of the English countryside. For the children of highly mobile international families, their boarding school may be the one constant in their globe-trotting lives.

International pupils bring benefits to the schools themselves. Academically, international students add a breadth of experience in the classroom which is invaluable in the social sciences. In language studies, the advantage of having bi- and trilingual children in a school is obvious. The cosmopolitan classroom prepares its pupils for life on a global stage. The result of all this is that international children are warmly welcomed at UK independent schools.

## The admissions process

The influx of international families has brought a greater flexibility in school admissions procedures. Dedicated international schools in large cities tend not to pursue the formal 11+ and 13+ entry procedures, but instead have a rolling admissions programme for international students, with individualised testing in the major subjects. The city independents, too, will often accommodate a strong international ▶

"We applied at very short notice, and were amazed to hear that the school was happy to consider us. As it was not possible for my children to visit the school to do the tests, they sent the tests to their schools in Hong Kong. These tests turned out to be seven one-hour exams in Reasoning, Maths and English! The kids survived and were accepted within days of the exams being returned to the school."

**GEOFF, PARENT OF AN 11-YEAR-OLD SON AND 13-YEAR-OLD DAUGHTER**

"No matter how you work it, applying from overseas is complicated, and the more so the more schools you apply for. The first complication was getting to see the schools, as visits generally have to be made during term time, and Hong Kong term times are similar to UK ones. In the end, we timed it for a non-overlapping half-term. As for exams, each school has different arrangements. One school was happy for my son to sit their exams under appropriate invigilation in Hong Kong, whereas the second required its exams to be taken in London. You need to be careful with exams, because syllabuses, topics and terminology can be different overseas. We then had to fly back for interviews—a trip for each. The schools could not make the interviews the same week, so we made four trips back and forth!"

**PETER, WHOSE SON APPLIED TO SELECTIVE LONDON SCHOOLS FROM HONG KONG AT 11+**

A boarding house at Handcross Park

applicant by way of exam procedures that differ from the procedures for local applicants. International applicants should be aware, however, that these schools are often heavily oversubscribed by local applicants and hence that their competition is a strong field of local children who are being prepared specifically for entry.

The majority of openings for international students will lie in the country boarding schools, which will do the most to try to accommodate international candidates, for example, by conducting private tours at times convenient to the parents or by setting exams that do not presume English as a first language. This flexibility will continue once the child is at the school: the school may, for example, arrange the child's curriculum to concentrate more heavily on certain subjects, or conduct parent/teacher exchanges by phone, rather than at the usual parents' evenings. In many schools, the system of 'exeat' weekends (weekends where boarders return home) has effectively been scrapped, so that children can take their weekends away as and when their parents can take them. The boarding houses will organise special activities—visits to cinemas and other attractions—for those who remain. ∎

## AUTHOR'S TIPS

# 6 THINGS TO CONSIDER IF APPLYING **FROM OVERSEAS**

**1** Find out the **number of international students** in the school. Ask also how many children usually remain in the boarding house over the weekend and how many remain during the course of the term. It is better to choose a school with a solid commitment to its students who board.

**2** Establish the percentage of **parents who regularly visit** or attend functions at the school. While there is no obligation on parents to be present at any particular event, your child may feel the distance more acutely if friends are receiving regular visits.

**3** Ask about the **support that international children are given** to help orientate them to British culture. A school with a reasonable international cohort might be expected to have a dedicated staff member to help international students.

**4** Consider the **qualifications** offered by the different schools. Depending on where you expect your child to attend university, the International Baccalaureate may be more widely recognised than A levels.

**5** Take particular note of the school's policy on the role of **UK-based guardians**. Some schools require the name and address of one or more guardians readily available to discuss with staff any issues or problems that may arise. Schools are unlikely to offer a place to a child where the guardianship arrangements are unsatisfactory.

**6** Bear in mind that, with the exception of the consulate and other bilingual schools, **tuition in the independent schools is in English**. Classes are fast-paced and children must be able to keep up.

Girl boarders at The Godolphin School

# Parenting

Finding the right school for your child is not always easy. Most parents who have been through the process of applying to independent schools report that they found it very challenging. From the preparation for exams to the wait for results, there will be moments of stress. Before anything else, it is worth considering how stressful the experience will be for you and for your child and in what ways.

monkeybusinessimages/iSTOCK/THINKSTOCK

## ASK YOURSELF...

... Are all family members in agreement about what sort of school will best suit your child? Might disagreements arise? If so, over what?

... Does my child agree with me on the sort of school that would best suit them? Are they willing to work with me to gain entry to such a school?

... How will my child respond to the stresses of the applications process? How will I respond? Are we as a family good at dealing with stress? How can I make it all a bit easier?

... How competitive are the schools we are interested in? If so, is it worth it? Should we opt for schools where admission will be less competitive?

... What are the chances of getting a bursary for my child? Do they have special skills that might attract an assisted place? Are there any bursaries for siblings, children of former puils or for members of a particular profession?

... What are our options for funding a school place if we do not obtain any assistance? How far are we prepared to go to afford it?

... Whose responsibility is this anyway? Who bears responsibility for your child's success? Your primary and prep school Heads will no doubt play an important role. However, it is you as parent who ultimately bears the responsibility for what happens to your child.

## TAKE THE PRESSURE OFF YOUR CHILD

Try to shield your child as best you can from the stress of the school admissions process. Be honest with your child and talk over your options, but do not let them feel that they will have failed if they do not gain entry to your chosen selective school.

## BEST TO REMEMBER ...

While your child's school will of course contribute hugely to their education, your own contribution will be greater. The quality of the parenting a child receives—the love, attention, support and encouragement—is a better indicator of future success than the quality of the child's school. A huge percentage of the students at Russell Group universities did not go to the 'best' schools. They went to perfectly standard schools, but were provided with opportunities through a combination of high aspirations and hard work. This is a winning combination that any child can foster, but it will of course be easier for a child who has the model supplied by their own parents to follow.

# HOW IMPORTANT IS CHOOSING THE RIGHT SCHOOL?

**Independent schools have very distinct characters, and so finding the right school for your child requires more than just looking at the top of the league tables.**

In the independent sector, parents have much greater flexibility about where they choose to send their child; you will not be limited by catchment areas, for example. You will also find a great level of variation between the schools, not only in their academic level, but in their atmosphere and ethos. A truism often repeated by school Heads is that there is no such thing as a good school, only a good school for your child. You alone can determine what makes for such a school.

Important as this decision is, try not to get swept up in all the advice you will be given about schools. As choosing the right school is such a personal decision, other people's advice may well not apply to you and your child. One particular factor to take with a pinch of salt is the importance of the league tables. While these appear, at first glance, to give a useful guide to the most successful schools, it is worth remembering that the schools on the league tables are not judged on an even field. Not all qualifications appear on all of the tables, and many schools actively choose not to share their information. League tables will tell you more about how the school selects its cohort than about the academic success it cultivates. Many excellent schools deliberately take children with a broad spread of academic abilities and so will not figure as highly on a league table, whereas a school that selects on academic ability alone, and culls students after GCSEs, will of course figure very highly.

## Choosing a pre-prep or prep school

At pre-prep and prep school level, the choice is arguably less important than at senior school. Many pre-prep and prep schools are populated by local children, rather than children who have specifically selected the school, therefore the spread of talents and temperaments of the children attending the school will be greater. You will nevertheless find that there are some significant differences between these schools in terms of their environment, facilities, atmosphere and educational priorities, as well as the levels of achievement expected of pupils. For example, some schools conduct formal

---

**HERE TO HELP**

"Is there anything the league tables are good for? No. They tell you little more than the academic entry requirements of a school. A highly selective school will inevitably top the league tables."

**JOHN BAUGH, HEADMASTER OF THE DRAGON SCHOOL**

---

Monkey Business Images/MONKEYBUSINESS/THINKSTOCK

## AUTHOR'S TIPS

# 4 FACTORS **NOT** TO CONSIDER (TOO GREATLY)

**1** **Other children's preferences.** While many children think they want to attend the same school as their friends, they may in fact welcome the chance to redefine themselves in a new school, away from the expectations of those who have known them since they were five.

**2** **Other people's opinions.** If you do intend to take someone's advice on a school, make sure that you share their criteria: what is 'too results-driven' to your friend may still be insufficiently academic to you, or vice versa.

**3** **The school's Head.** The chances of a Head remaining until the end of your child's time at the school are not high.

**4** **The league tables.** League tables cannot be used to predict the future success of your child at a school, and less still their future happiness.

exams from the youngest years, and some may stream or 'set' children in certain subjects (though even some of the highest-achieving preps will not do this).

One of the most important differences to consider between prep schools is their age range: does the school continue to Year 6 or Year 8? If you are considering applying to a senior school that has its major intake at 13+, check that the prep school actually continues to age 13. If not, what is involved in making the change at 11+? You may decide that, if your child is to sit Common Entrance or other exams at 13+, it would be better if they did not also need to sit exams at 11+. Opinions differ on this question: on the one hand, competitive exams at 11+ may give your child skills for the 13+ round; on the other, you may feel it is extra stress that a child of this age simply does not need.

### Choosing a senior school

At senior level, the differences between the schools are much more pronounced than in earlier years. Particularly in boarding schools, children may travel long distances for a particular school's emphasis on sport, or their unique curriculum, or their distinctive ethos—and so you will find schools populated with a high proportion of pupils who reflect these characteristics. There are schools best suited for sporty students, schools best

suited for highly studious students, schools for pupils with a particular gift in music or drama, schools for the less academic.

Each school will be looking for children to fit its particular ethos, and they will base their entrance criteria on a combination of factors, from academic level to personality traits. In choosing a school, therefore, you will also want to consider various factors, such as the destination of school leavers, the relationship between teachers and pupils, the size of the school, its facilities in the area of particular interest to you, and so on. ▶

morrolight/ISTOCK/THINKSTOCK

# AUTHOR'S TIPS

# 15 FACTORS TO CONSIDER
# WHEN CHOOSING A SCHOOL

**1** **Academic results.** The first job of a school is, after all, to educate.

**2** **The destination of school leavers.** At prep level, look at the senior schools that students move on to; at senior level, look at the universities. Note: it is worth finding out whether the pupils achieving the best university offers are long-standing pupils, or those the school has imported into the Sixth Form to improve its academic profile.

**3** **Curriculum and qualifications.** The most significant difference here is between A levels and the International Baccalaureate. **(For more on A levels and IB, see p. 104.)** Other differences include a preference for Cambridge Pre-U courses over A levels, or IGCSE over GCSE courses. You may also find differences in the availability of subjects.

**4** **Atmosphere, character and ethos.** The ethos of a school will influence the attitudes and values your child adopts during this formative period of their life. It will influence your child's chances of success, by influencing their attitude to hard work and achievement.

**5** **Friendliness and approachability of staff.** A child needs teachers whom they respect and have confidence in; equally, a child needs to feel that the teachers respect and have confidence in them.

**6** **Environment and facilities.** The environment of a school will inevitably be one of the key elements in your child's enjoyment of it— especially in a boarding school.

**7** **Size.** Some children are more suited to a small, friendly school, where each child ends up knowing every other child's name. Others will prefer the variety of having a huge cohort around them.

**8** **Prestige.** Some of the UK's top schools have such a worldwide reputation that simply having their name on your child's CV will help them.

**9** **The priority given to sport.** Some schools will place great importance on team sports and success in competitions, and have brilliant results to show for it. Consider the level of participation in the various sports: is it the same for boys and girls? Are there C and D teams, besides A and B teams?

**10** **The priority given to the creative arts.** A school that encourages participation in the creative arts will offer plenty of avenues for involvement: school plays, form plays, a large choir, regular concerts and a range of exhibitions, and so forth. Ask about the policies the school adopts to encourage participation.

**11** **The breadth and quality of extra-curricular activities.** School trips are often the highlight of a child's senior schooling, but some schools offer far fewer than others. There should also be a healthy range of clubs: aerobics, zumba, chess, cooking, debating, pottery, philosophy... Try to ascertain the level of participation in these clubs.

**12** **Location.** If a great deal of time will be spent travelling to and from school, remember that this time will be relatively unproductive. And do not underrate the stress added to a school day by unreliable transport.

**13** **Qualifications of teaching staff.** At a good independent school, you would expect the teaching staff to have qualifications beyond a basic degree.

**14** **The school's pupils.** Of all aspects of school life, your child will be influenced most directly by the children they interact with on a day-to-day level. What is the demeanour of these children? How do they behave towards each other? Would you be pleased to see your child amongst them?

**15** **Sense of social responsibility.** Check what the school is doing to accommodate children from less privileged backgrounds, and what opportunities there are for your child to volunteer in outreach programmes at the higher years. Many children find volunteering to be a fun and rewarding experience.

PHOTOS: TOP, OAKHAM SCHOOL. BOTTOM PERFORMING ARTS FACILITIES AT SEVENOAKS SCHOOL

# HOW DO I FIND OUT ABOUT SCHOOLS?

*The process of finding out about schools and applying to them can be arduous: there are simply so many schools.*

**W**hen you are starting out in your school search, the best advice may be to gather information on schools from every source available. In the early stages of your research, do not put too much store by any single piece of advice given to you about a particular school, whatever its source. You need to find out for yourself.

Many people embark on their school search by way of a web search. If you conduct a web search of independent schools in the UK, however, you will soon find yourself overwhelmed with choice. Besides selecting by region, you will need to narrow down the number of schools that interest you. Beyond the geographical, the most obvious differences between the schools are that some offer boarding while others do not, some are co-educational while others are single-sex, and some offer A levels while others offer the International Baccalaureate. There are a number of good ways to research schools more closely, in order to determine which interest you. ■

## AUTHOR'S TIPS

# 11 WAYS TO GET INFORMATION ABOUT SCHOOLS

**1 School websites.** You will learn a great deal about a school from its website: its curriculum, admissions procedure, leavers' grades, destinations, fees, and so on. Usually there is a message from the Head outlining their vision for the school.

**2 School magazines.** The school's magazine, sent on request or available at open days, will tell you about the activities the pupils take part in.

**3 School reports.** A school's report provides a wealth of information on provision of education and care. Schools are required to make their most recent report available; this can usually be found on a school's website.

**4 Independent Schools Association websites.** The most useful sites are the Independent Schools Council (ISC), the Scottish Council of Independent Schools (SCIS), and the Headmasters' and Headmistresses' Conference (HMC). For preps, try the Independent Association of Prep Schools (IAPS); for boarding schools, the Boarding Schools Association (BSA); for girls' schools, the Girls' Schools Association (GSA).

**5 Independent publications.** The Good Schools Guide is the best known of these. It contains information and reviews of over 1100 of the UK's top schools, which are informative and impartial.

**6 Independent websites.** Several independent companies have websites where you can conduct school searches, including: The Good Schools Guide, Independent Schools of the British Isles (isbi), best-schools.co.uk and ukboardingschools.com.

**7 School exhibitions.** The Independent Schools Show is staged in London every year and in various cities overseas. Many schools set up booths and have staff members on hand, including Heads and Registrars.

**8 Private consultancies.** Several companies will advise you on choice of school, including The Good Schools Guide Advisory Service. Make sure any agency is not being paid for recommending a school, and do not pay for a 'guaranteed place'; these will likely be at schools for which entry would not be difficult. Note: It may not be in your best interests for agencies to approach schools on your behalf.

**9 Pupils and parents.** Pupils often know more about their school than anyone else. Ask your present school if they can put you in touch with the parents of former pupils now at the schools that interest you.

**10 Forums.** Mumsnet.com has a general schools forum, and the Independent Junction website has a forum for independent school parents.

**11 The school's open day.** A school visit is the most valuable source of information of all. **(See p. 28.)**

*We recommend...*

# THE GOOD SCHOOLS GUIDE

For nearly 30 years the Good Schools Guide has offered independent, unbiased and forthright advice from experts on all aspects of choosing a school. They review schools from a parent's perspective, answering the questions that help you decide if a particular school would be right for your child.

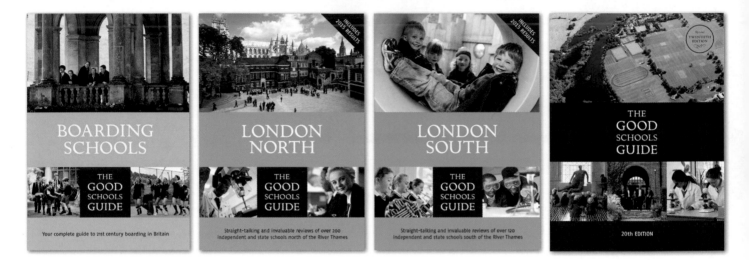

## 'How can we decide when every school looks perfect?'

When planning your child's education you can never have too much information, but selecting the right independent school can be a daunting prospect. Schools now market themselves so professionally that parents tell us they feel overwhelmed by glossy prospectuses and slick websites. Good Schools Guide reviews start where the prospectus stops, giving you inside information, parent views, academic profiles and much, much more. Our guide is full of good schools; our reviews will help lead you to the one that is best for your child.

In addition to *The Good Schools Guide*, now in its 20th year and covering schools nationally (available from the Good Schools Guide website for £39.95), the company also publishes stand-alone guides to the best state and independent schools in London: *The Good Schools Guide London South* and *The Good Schools Guide London North* (£18 each), as well as *The Good Schools Guide — Boarding Schools*, covering the UK's best boarding schools (£22).

Get in touch: 0203 286 6824
www.goodschoolsguide.co.uk

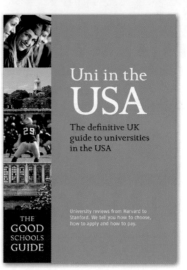

They also publish *Uni in the USA and Beyond*, a comprehensive guide to the hugely varied American higher education sector. Reviews are written by funny, sharp-eyed British students and cover not only the USA but also selected universities in Europe, China, Canada and Australia. *Uni in the USA and Beyond* is available as a paperback (£18) or online.
www.uniintheusa.com

## The Good Schools Guide online

With a subscription to the Good Schools Guide website you can customise your school search to your family's circumstances using their advanced search features. Subscribers have access to all the Good Schools Guide's opinionated, detailed and informative reviews and can augment these by drawing on their unparalleled wealth of statistics and data, including most recent exam results. In addition, subscribers have full access to hundreds of informative articles on all aspects of education, not to mention the Good Schools Guide's popular blog. Subscriptions start at £15 for one month.

If you're looking for an international school for your child you'll want to subscribe to The Good Schools Guide International, which covers top international schools catering to English speaking expats in over 55 countries worldwide.

## The Good Schools Guide Advice Service

You may have done all your school research, planned ahead and put your child's name down for a school in good time but then the unexpected happens: a new job; moving to a different country; discovering your child has dyslexia... If for any reason you find yourself having to start the school search again from scratch or under time pressure, the Good Schools Guide experts can help.

The Good Schools Guide Advice Service (GSGAS) is a personal service for families covering every aspect of schools and education. Their experienced advisors have visited countless schools, and quizzed innumerable parents, children, teachers and head teachers. This vast experience, coupled with local knowledge, inside information and the shared expertise of the entire team, is available to GSGAS clients.

Because GSGAS is a personal service, run on a one-to-one basis, they can help you in whatever way you need, be that a 30 minute telephone or Skype conversation, face-to-face advice, accompanied school visits, educational assessments—the list goes on.

GSGAS can also offer specialised advice on all aspects of SEN education, on scholarships and bursaries, and even a dedicated London service.

**www.goodschoolsguide.co.uk/advice**

# WHAT SHOULD I LOOK OUT FOR ON A SCHOOL TOUR?

**The only sure way to ascertain whether a school is right for your child is to visit it, maybe more than once.**

Blundell's Chapel Musicans

The standard practice for visits to a school by prospective parents is for an initial visit on an open day and then a further, booked school tour when the school is in operation, either singly or in groups. Make sure you book early for these tours or you may find that you miss the opportunity. The school can only schedule so many tours during the year, and they fill up fast. Many schools, particularly boarding schools, will conduct individual tours at other times, to suit parents.

You will make better use of a school visit if you have done basic research beforehand, so that you do not waste time on questions easily answered by a trip to the school's website. Establish in advance the size and history of the school, its facilities, curriculum, public exam results, the general outlines of the admissions process, and so on. Then use the school visit as a way of finding out about the underlying nature of the school, and the type of child to whom it is best suited. These visits provide an

opportunity to meet the members of staff who will play an important role in your child's life.

## Open days

A parent's first visit to a school is often an open day. Usually, the Head will speak about the character of the school and explain the admissions process; a prefect or other pupil will also usually speak, and sometimes also a parent. A tour of the school will be given, often conducted by a pupil. The disadvantage of the open day is that the school is trying to impress, so everyone will be better-dressed and better-behaved than usual. Work will be available to peruse; exhibits will be on the walls and in the art rooms; the school choir or orchestra may present a short concert. The school will be trying to show itself at its best: the smell of flowers in vases and brownies cooking in the kitchens will hang in the air. The advantage of the open days is that it gives you an opportunity to address questions to a pupil

or a parent of the school. If there is a parent speaker, ask how they find the school and its pupils, and if there is anything that they are less happy with. You can even ask for advice on making an application to the school: what type of child does the school look for?

Even if you do not get the opportunity to ask questions, there is still much that can be gleaned simply by observing a school: by looking at the classrooms, the facilities and so on. Pay particular attention to the noticeboards: there should be a wealth of information about clubs, sporting activities, concerts, school trips and so on. There may be a board celebrating what pupils are achieving outside the school. Look at the displays in the classrooms: are they inspiring? Look at the fabric of the school, particularly the science labs and IT suite, to see whether it is well-maintained. Pay close attention to the library: is it a pleasant place to spend time? Are the books being read? Do they support the

Art facilities at Bedales

Cricket facilities at Cranleigh

subjects on the curriculum? And lastly, look at the children themselves: do they appear to be happy and proud to show off their school? In a vibrant school, the children will appear happy, confident, proud of their school and pleased to speak well of it. They will appear enthusiastic about their studies and their extra-curricular activities. (Enthusiasm is difficult for a child to simulate, so if they appear to be enthusiastic, they probably are.)

At some point, it is good to speak to the Registrar or Admissions staff in person. If you are very interested in a school and are registering for it, then it would also be good if, by the time of your exams, the Registrar could put a face to your name.

## Bringing your child to the school

There may be an advantage in taking a preliminary tour of a school without your child: you do not want your child to fall in love with a school that, for one reason or another, you do not want them to attend. However, at some point your child must certainly join you in visiting the schools for which you register. Your child may then start to appreciate what is at stake in exam preparation, and in turn the school will gauge your interest in them. When it comes to your child's interview, they can fully expect the question: 'When you came to visit the school,

is there anything you particularly liked about it?' If your child hasn't visited the school, there will be nothing to talk about. If they have, then of course the correct answer is 'Yes!'—with evidence to support it. Naturally, a school will be more inclined to make an offer where they know it will be accepted.

## Preparing for problems

Because you will naturally be feeling optimistic when you visit these schools, it may not occur to you to ask an important question: what happens when things go wrong? You want to know how the school tracks progress, for example, and how they identify if your child is not progressing. Some schools have sophisticated tracking using a value-added system, and can pick up when your child is not making progress within a term. You also want to know what would happen were your child to be bullied in any way. Bullying can happen to any child, even the most amiable, and there should be effective measures in place to deal with it. Do not be satisfied by the claim that 'bullying does not happen in this school'. It happens everywhere.

## Getting the details

You may need to visit a school that particularly interests you more than once to cover some of these areas. A first visit will give you a

feel for the school and answer the general questions you may have. A second visit will give you a closer look at the day-to-day working of the school and establish whether it will work for your child. For this visit, formulate a list of questions that are specific to your circumstances: are other children coming from my area to the school? How do they get back and forth from school? Are they encouraged to go on public transport together? Is there a school bus service? Is it reliable? Give thought, in advance, to issues which need to be addressed in person. Your aim by the end of the visit is to be in a position to decide whether you are interested in registering for that school. ∎

### HERE TO HELP

"It is important that families come to the right decision based on informed knowledge, first-hand experience and a clear understanding of the ethos of the school. At open days, note whether the school looks tidy, whether there is plenty going on (according to noticeboards), whether the pupils interact well with the staff and show good manners towards you, and whether there is a general 'buzz' around the school. Try not to be too analytical, but pay attention to your gut reaction."

**MARK JOHNSON, HEADMASTER OF CHEAM**

Nursery pupils at L'Ecole des Petits in Chelsea

# SHOULD MY CHILDREN GO TO THE SAME SCHOOL?

**While sending your children to the same school is certainly convenient, one school may not perfectly suit all members of the family.**

There are practical benefits to sending your children to the same school, such as ease of travelling to and from school. A commitment to the one school will minimise the demands on your time: you will not need to attend parallel speech days, concerts, sports days and so on—and you will not need to juggle schedule clashes. You may be surprised to discover that, irritatingly, term dates vary among schools, so that a two-week holiday period may spin out to three weeks or more when your children attend different schools. This can be a serious issue for working parents. It is also worth bearing in mind that a school with a policy of giving preference to siblings will simplify your job when it comes to later admissions. There may also be deeper advantages to being a 'single school family', in that family bonds are built by way of shared experiences of schooling.

Against these considerations, you might weigh these: will all your children thrive in the same environment or will they do better at schools tailored to their differing natures and educational needs? It is not unusual to have children in the one family whose academic, sporting and creative skills vary markedly or whose psychological and emotional needs likewise differ. It may do younger children a great disservice to try to fit them into the mould created by the first. In short, the single-school policy limits your choices, especially if you have both a boy and a girl and must therefore choose a co-educational school. ∎

> "While every child should go to the school that is right for them—socially and academically—it is much easier if your children attend the same school. My sons' school is very good at treating them as individuals, but there is educational continuity—and it's comforting for them to know the other is there! In addition, coordination of parents' evenings, sports fixtures and other school events is much easier."
>
> **JILL,** MOTHER OF TWIN BOYS AT A LONDON DAY SCHOOL

> "It's all about horses for courses. One of my children wanted to board, the other one didn't—and it's worked out brilliantly. Although they are incredibly close, they can be their individual selves in separate schools."
>
> **JOEY,** MOTHER OF A SON AND DAUGHTER SIX YEARS APART

# HOW IMPORTANT IS THE
# RELIGIOUS FOUNDATION
## OF A SCHOOL?

Many independent schools have a religious foundation, but the impact of this religion on daily school life may not be huge.

Downside
Catholic Co-Ed
Boarding School

If applying for independent schools in the UK, you should be aware that many of them have a historical association with the Church of England which has gone on for centuries. While they are affiliated with the Church, and often have chapels, they do not require children to belong to the Church of England to be considered for entry. The websites of these schools make this clear, in words such as: 'This school accepts applications from children of all faiths, and indeed, none.'

Applicants for these schools should be aware, however, that the religion of these schools is Christian and the prevailing culture is broadly Anglican. The children will commonly attend church services, participate in religious worship, celebrate Christian festivals, receive Anglican sermons and may study Religious Education from an Anglican perspective. While children may be given some latitude in the level of their involvement in actual worship, participation in the church services may not be optional; they are part of the normal running of the school. If this is a problem for you, you will need to ask the school what religious involvement is required of its pupils. You may wish to ask for specific details, such as whether children are required to sing hymns.

That said, these schools are multi-faith communities, welcoming children of many different creeds and a large cohort of children with no religious affiliation at all. This raises a further issue: these schools are places of education and so welcome debate on religion, as on any other issue. Whatever their faith, children are expected to hold informed and reasoned debate on religious matters, without causing or taking affront. Parents must be sensitive to religious diversity as well, considering any dietary restrictions your child's friends may have, for example. This is of course the case in any school in the UK. ∎

> "If you wish your child to develop their faith outside the home, then choose a school where access to religious activities is compulsory and frequent. Laziness and peer pressure are inherent in adolescence, and without regular direction and encouragement your child may develop indifference in an increasing secular world. So ask detailed questions and make contact with the relevant faith leader as part of your selection process."
>
> **PETER**, FATHER OF DAUGHTER AT A CATHOLIC SCHOOL

> "When we chose the school for our daughter, we were aware that it was a Christian school. Our daughter did have to go to chapel and we got a bit of grumbling about that from her, as we do not go to church as a family. With top schools like this chapel is part of the package, but there was certainly no indoctrination."
>
> **MATTHEW**, FATHER OF DAUGHTER AT A CHURCH OF ENGLAND SCHOOL

# IS A BOARDING SCHOOL ?
# RIGHT FOR MY CHILD ?

**Whether or not to send your child to a boarding school is a decision that will affect the whole family.**

Boarder working in her room at Cranleigh

The strongest arguments for boarding schools are the time and space they allow pupils. With facilities on site, time spent in transit is freed up for more worthwhile activities. These boarding schools are often set in acres of land, with playing fields, gardens, lakes, vegetable patches, farms and so on. For some boarding children, the tranquillity of the setting, free from urban distractions, is a major factor in their success at school.

These schools also offer qualified staff on hand to support the child's work; the teacher-student bonds formed in boarding schools may contribute significantly to a child's education.

Lastly, boarding schools offer a vast array of activities and friends with whom to enjoy them. Homework becomes part of the daily routine. So too, with other activities available to boarders: a child will give things a go in a boarding school which they may not do otherwise. So children learn independence in

# AUTHOR'S TIPS

## 3 CONCERNS ABOUT BOARDING – AND WHY YOU SHOULDN'T WORRY

**1** For tightly-knit families, the loss of a child for weeks at a time may seem unbearable. However, children are no longer obliged to go for weeks without seeing their parents. **Parental involvement** is encouraged wherever possible: parents attend sports events, concerts, social events and so on, just as in a day school.

*Photo: Boarding facilities at the Bethany School*

**2** Shy children, solitary children and children with a particular love of their home life may find the hubbub of a boarding school difficult. Although many children do feel homesick or overwhelmed at times, they provide a great **support network** for each other, and will be well looked after by house 'parents': older pupils who play a role in mentoring younger children. Boarding school teaches children how to live and share with each other—and children are given a lot more privacy than you'd expect.

**3** Parents fear that their **relationships with their children** will suffer if they board. In fact, the opposite tends to happen: the time parents spend with their children is free from the pressure of school routine (and arguments about homework!).

a structured, supportive environment and they emerge from their boarding schools as mature and confident young people.

The best advice for any parent struggling with this question is to explore the options at first hand. Any abstract discussion of the benefits of a boarding school amounts to little when compared to visiting a boarding school and looking at how the children live in their houses and what they do on a day-to-day level. Many parents who would never have considered a boarding school are won over by what they see if they chance to visit one.

PHOTO: PIKSEL/ iSTOCK/ THINKSTOCK

### Is there a compromise?

Some parents try for a solution that keeps both options in play. There is now much greater

### THIS MAY HELP

The Good Schools Guide — Boarding Schools is a book dedicated to finding the best boarding school for your child.

---

flexibility in boarding arrangements than there used to be: the choice of full boarding, weekly boarding and flexi-boarding is offered in many schools. Some allow families to switch between full and weekly boarding as circumstances dictate. What's more, the benefits of boarding are shared by day pupils in these schools: the arrangements for day pupils mirror the 'house' system, giving children a 'day house' to return to in breaks, complete with housemasters/ mistresses to ensure the pupils' well-being. At some schools, there is 'home boarding', where day pupils have supper and do their prep with the regular boarders, heading home at about 9 pm. If you are considering boarding at a later stage, either for the child applying or for later siblings, such a school may postpone the need to make a final decision. ∎

## HOW I FOUND...

### MY BOARDING SCHOOL EXPERIENCE

"My happiest memories of boarding come from the strong feeling we had of all being in it together. We would never let any of our friends get in trouble, even if it meant lying through our teeth to the matrons! The friendships I made at boarding school remain the strongest friendships in my life. The school made the settling in process very easy. My first week was filled with activities designed to help us bond with our peers and learn the school inside out. Within a few days, we'd pulled together and put on a play! Boarding was an incredible experience for me, but obviously it won't be happy all the time. Almost every child gets homesick at some point, and I'm sure it must be hard for parents to be so far away when their child calls home in tears. But just know: nine times out of ten, half an hour after your child is crying down the phone, they're bouncing around their dorm without a care in the world, while their poor parents are left worrying for nothing!"

**Emma, former pupil at a country girls' boarding school**

The Godolphin School, an all-girls boarding school

# SHOULD WE CHOSE A CO-ED OR SINGLE SEX SCHOOL?

There are excellent schools across the UK of each type, so there is no clear argument either way, but some parents may find this aspect of school life important.

**Girls at independent girls' schools are 1.5 times more likely to study Physics at A level than girls at independent co-educational schools.**

From research by the Institute of Physics

## The argument for single sex schools

The top of the league tables are dominated by schools that are single sex: at a recent count, seven of the ten most highly achieving independent schools in this country were single sex schools—and five of these were girls' schools. Girls at single sex schools are more strongly encouraged to take subjects such as Maths and Science, which they then go on to excel at, whereas at co-educational schools these subjects are often seen as being 'for boys', and so the girls avoid them. If the presence of boys means that girls are being put off studying hard sciences, you may rightly

wonder about the broader impact of boys in the classroom on your daughter's education. The independent girls' schools are particularly good at encouraging high aspirations in their girls, on the assumption that every subject is a 'girls' subject'.

A related argument can be made in favour of boys' schools. Since boys mature later than girls, they need steering through their teens, to encourage social and moral maturity. In recent years, evidence has also emerged that some boys are put off doing well in an academic arena where they feel they may be outshone by girls. Clearly, both sexes need an environment where they can achieve without being self-conscious about their perceived roles in relation to the other sex.

## The argument for co-educational schools

Segregated schools are often seen as a relic of former days, happily receding into the past. Indeed, since many of the old public schools

### STRAIGHT FROM THE HORSE'S MOUTH

"The independent sector gives parents choice. For some parents, that leads to a single sex school where, in the important teenage years, students are free from distractions or unfair competition. In girls' schools, girls lead as prefects—and they choose subjects according to career choice, enjoyment or abilities, not through gender stereotyping. Girls don't pick up subliminal messages that boys may be more important: 'We'll do the rugby results first then the netball'. It is crucial for girls and boys to mix, so joint lectures, debates and social events like barbecues are a normal part of the school week. In this environment, strong boys- and girls-only schools see their pupils thrive personally and academically."

**MARY BREEN,** HEADMISTRESS OF ST MARY'S SCHOOL ASCOT

Pupils take a break outside Blundell's, a co-ed school

have become co-educational in the past few decades, girls can now enjoy the facilities and prestige that were once the sole preserve of boys. For the parents of girls, this alone may be enough to convince them of the merits of

## MY SINGLE SEX SCHOOL

"I do think I benefitted academically from being at a single sex school. There was no culture of trying to impress, and the focus was on work. However, my social skills did suffer to an extent. When I went to university, it was initially tricky to manage friendships with boys, as I just wasn't used to it."

**Sophie, former boarder in an all-girls country boarding school**

co-education. There are wider benefits: co-educational schools provide for a healthy, well-balanced social setting in which the talents of all can be celebrated. The talents traditionally proper to one sex can be pursued precisely because they are beneficial to the other: lessons in confidence and self-assertion are exchanged for lessons in diligence and organisation. Increasing numbers of parents are opting for co-educational schools for these reasons.

The numbers of co-educational schools is on the rise in the UK, mainly due to the fact that many single sex schools have become co-educational in recent decades. This is particularly true in the upper years. A number of schools now offer single sex teaching until Year 11 and a co-educational Sixth Form in Years 12 and 13. Note, however, that the ratio of the sexes in these schools may not be 50:50, unlike in the established co-educational sector. A further development is the so-called diamond model, operating in a number of co-educational schools, where children are taught

in co-educational classes until Year 6, single sex classes from Years 7–11 and co-educational classes again in Sixth Form. The children in these schools benefit from the best of both worlds, as it were. ■

### STRAIGHT FROM THE HORSE'S MOUTH

"Life is co-educational, and it is our responsibility as educators to prepare children for the world in which they will live. It's also vital to acknowledge that children (not genders) have different learning styles and good teachers make lessons accessible, engaging and challenging to all their pupils. Truly co-ed schools, such as Oakham (with 50% boys and 50% girls) are gender equal environments that enable all pupils to choose and develop their talents, irrespective of their gender."

**NIGEL LASHBROOK, HEADMASTER OF OAKHAM SCHOOL**

# SHOULD WE AIM FOR A HIGHLY ACADEMIC SCHOOL?

**Academic success is not as simple as attending the most academic school.**

The schools that top the league tables are among the best in the world. But if your child does not fit the academic profile of these schools, they may find themselves languishing in the bottom set. Do not be under any misapprehension about the standards expected at these schools: in some, over half of the pupils will achieve 10 A*s at GCSE (a 1 or 2 on the new scale). Such a school does not look on a B in a public exam with any sympathy. Some schools have years of unbroken records of A/A* grades; imagine being the child who fears breaking that record. Bear in mind also that some schools cull students during the senior years. For some children, the prospect of losing their place at the school will certainly be an incentive to work hard; for others it will be a source of stress. Many pupils at these schools put in hours of homework simply because they enjoy it, so consider whether your child fits the profile socially as well as academically.

These schools are not the 'hot-houses' described in some sections of the media; they are truly excellent schools which foster the 'whole child' approach to education. However, the most academic school will not necessarily bring out the best in your child. Ideally your child would be in the middle of the range of academic ability, so they are stimulated by the more able to reach a higher academic level without losing self-esteem by being at the bottom. If your child attends a school that suits

their academic level, they may have a better chance of gaining entrance to a top university. You should try, therefore, to establish the academic level of your child—being as candid with yourself as optimism allows. But how do you make such an assessment?

## How your current school can help

If your child is in a state school, their teacher will tell you whether they are on track to reach the upper level or band at KS2, which independent schools generally expect at 11+. Primary schools carry out these assessments regularly and there should be no problem obtaining this information.

If your child is at a prep school, ask the teachers about how they are performing in school assessments and about their position in the class. This information will, of course, be useful only if you know whether the cohort as a whole is strong or weak. If your child attends a large prep school with a varied cohort, then their ranking will provide useful information. On the basis of past experience, the prep school should know the academic level expected of children at various schools. Find out from your prep school where your child will likely sit.

Prep schools also assess a child's potential by conducting CAT tests. The most recent versions show their relative strength in four areas of reasoning: Verbal, Non-verbal, Quantitative and Spatial. Schools often seem reluctant to share the results of these tests with parents but you can always ask about them. The average score for these tests is 100. The most academically selective schools will be looking for a CAT test score of 120 or higher, which correlates with the attainment of the highest grades at GCSE.

## Testing academic achievement at home

If you are still unsure, download some specimen examination papers for 11+ or 13+ entry, many of which are made available by

### THIS MAY HELP

Visit www.independentjunction.co.uk to find the relevant specimen exam papers.

schools on their websites. The marks your child obtains in these specimen papers may then be used to assess your child's suitability for prospective schools. You can ask Registrars to tell you the sort of marks that successful applicants have achieved in these papers in the past. (They may or may not tell you.)

Bear in mind that if your child does intensive exam preparation, their marks may improve dramatically. (Parents commonly speak of 20–25% increases in children's marks over the course of six months or so.) If a child is of average academic attainment but devotes months to exam preparation, they can apply for schools further up the academic scale. Note, however, that if your child is judged on marks inflated by intensive preparation, they will remain under constant pressure to maintain these marks throughout their senior schooling. ∎

## HOW I FOUND...

### MY LESS ACADEMIC SCHOOL

"My school wasn't overly academic, and as somebody with interests spread all over the place, I benefitted hugely from this. I was in the choir, did tech for school plays, played sports, received my Gold Duke of Edinburgh Award, on top of doing well at exams. At a less academically focused school, I was allowed to be all of these things and more."

**Alice, former pupil at a country boarding school**

---

### STRAIGHT FROM THE HORSE'S MOUTH

"My advice to parents looking for a senior school is this: find a school where their child will not 'bump along the bottom'; that offers opportunities that fit with their child's interests and ambitions; and that gives them academic ambition and high expectations if and when they start to push on academically."

**JOHN BAUGH,** HEADMASTER OF THE DRAGON SCHOOL

Bedales'
impressive
Memorial
Library

## AUTHOR'S
# TIPS

# COULD A HIGHLY ACADEMIC SCHOOL
# HINDER OXBRIDGE CHANCES?

When it comes to university admissions, the pupils of the most selective schools are competing against each other for entry to the top universities—and this can be an unpleasant experience for a child who is not as accomplished as their friends. The schools on the top of the league tables have selected their cohort as potential Oxbridge candidates all along. In some schools, the majority apply to Oxbridge and each applicant will have the marks and the ability to succeed there. But there are limits to the numbers that can reasonably be taken from any single school.

There are various effects of this: a highly selective school will know that it can do little to improve its Oxbridge numbers, so it may provide less help to its Oxbridge applicants than the schools eager to improve their Oxbridge numbers. Indeed, knowing that each Oxbridge college will likely take only one child from the school in a given field, the school may be reluctant to support too many applications. But whose application will it be? Naturally, the most accomplished pupils will have earned the right to their first choice. This experience can be demoralising for the child at the bottom of the school—even though this child will likely attain an A average. The problem is that their friends will attain A*.

# MY CHILD HAS SEN: WHERE SHOULD WE APPLY?

**The UK is one of the best educators of children with Special Educational Needs (SEN) in the world —yet many schools do not even advertise the fact that they have facilities for children with SEN.**

It is now increasingly recognised that the number of children with SEN is far greater than formerly thought. It is also recognised that having SEN does not correlate either with intelligence or a lack of it. Many schools will conduct testing in the first year of their pupils' entry into the school and repeat it at later stages as well, thereby discovering children with SEN who were previously undiagnosed.

Within the independent school sector are dedicated SEN schools, with pupils who share specific learning difficulties. More commonly, however, independent schools aim to support a child with SEN within the mainstream school environment. To that end, schools have programmes for pupils with SEN and teachers who are qualified and experienced in overseeing these programmes. Individual educational plans—with details of extra learning support to be provided—are commonplace, with a dedicated teacher whose responsibility it is to ensure that the aims of the plan are met. The schools will also be aware of what can be done to ensure that children with SEN are accommodated in the public examinations and will support applications for a child to work on a computer or be given extra time in these exams. Prospective parents should inquire about what services are available at the school, and what additional costs they may incur.

If your child has a clinical diagnosis of any special need, approach the Registrar and/or

> **Over 66,000 pupils from schools in the Independent Schools Council are identified as having Special Educational Needs, of which the most common is dyslexia.**
>
> Taken from the Independent Schools Council website

> "When your child has special needs, selecting a school requires extra care and research. Doctors, therapists and special education teachers may be able to advise on schools to consider. For some children, it will be clear that a school for children with disabilities is the best choice; for others, a mainstream school is better. Look for a school which truly welcomes your child, which will make a commitment to developing their potential, and which will deliver the curriculum in a form modified to suit them. Teachers should initiate frequent communication about your child's progress. Some children with special needs are vulnerable to bullying and abuse. It is important to look for a school with a strong anti-bullying policy which is rigorously enforced."
>
> **SUSANNE, WHOSE TWO DAUGHTERS ATTENDED INDEPENDENT SCHOOLS**

Kathy Yeulet/HEMERA/THINKSTOCK

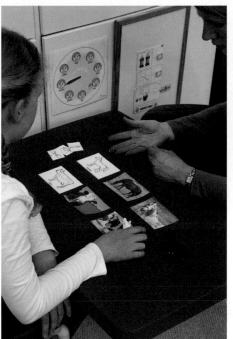

Macsnap/iSTOCK/THINKSTOCK

the exams to which your child is best suited. Dyslexic children may perform less well in reasoning tests and so be advised to pursue schools which do not rely on such tests at entry. Other children may not score well in the CAT tests at 11+, for instance, and so be advised to seek entry to a school which conducts its own tests at 13+, which highlight other strengths your child may have. ∎

## THESE MAY HELP

Independent Parental Special Education Advice (IPSEA) is a national charity providing free and independent information, advice and support to help get the right education for children with all kinds of special educational needs (SEN) and disabilities: www.ipsea.org.uk.

Information for parents of children with SEN can also be found at the website of the Independent Schools Inspectorate (ISI): www.isi.co.uk/information-for-parents/special-educational-needs.

The Good Schools Guide Advice Service offers expert advice in placing children with SEN. They also offer an SEN Surgery Helpline for quick advice on 0203 286 6824.

Head in person to discuss your situation in detail. The school will typically ask for a full report from an educational psychologist to be appended to your initial registration. (This will probably cost around £700–800. It will need to be updated prior to major public exams.) This will help the school identify the challenges your child has faced in their achievements to date. Having considered the report, the staff will be in a better position to advise you about the level of support the school can provide and the costs you may incur. Beyond this, you will also want to establish that the school has an atmosphere and an ethos which will allow your child to flourish.

## Tackling admissions with SEN

The psychologist's report should also explain any irregularities in your child's performance in the admissions exams. Individual schools may be inclined to vary their standard admissions procedures on the basis of a psychologist's report that suggests a child cannot present themselves at their best by way of the procedures currently in place. A school may also stake less on the exam results than on the interview, especially if they see in the child that 'spark' that these schools tend to favour.

Otherwise, you may need to concentrate your efforts on the schools that conduct

Macsnap/iSTOCK/THINKSTOCK

# Parenting

Try to get your child involved in and excited about the admissions process. Together with your child and other members of your family, work out the parameters of what you are looking for in a school. Then, set your child the task of choosing a handful of schools to visit. Ask your child what they like about each of these schools and what you should look out for when you get there. If your child is to be committed to the admissions process, they must feel that they've had an input in the decision-making, and confident that their concerns may be voiced.

Mark Bowden/ISTOCK/THINKSTOCK

## LOOK AT YOUR CHILD

If you are unsure which type of school you should be considering, look at your child's strengths and weaknesses. What type of school would serve them best? What works at your child's present school and what does not?

## ASK YOURSELF...

Why exactly would you like your child to attend this or that school?

## ASK YOURSELF...

What will matter most to my child during their time at the school?

## GIVE EACH SCHOOL ITS MERITS

If you are aiming for one school and treating a second as back-up, do not tell your child. Consider the impact on your child's later schooling if they suspect that their school is second best. Find a reason to prefer every school that you apply for.

## ENCOURAGE YOUR CHILD TO THINK CRITICALLY

While you are discussing the schools you will visit with your child, encourage them to think critically: Is it really possible to commute to this school or will it take too long? Will the children really play as much sport if they need to be ferried by bus to the sports field? If your child shows a marked preference for one school over another, do not take this judgement at face value. Ask for reasons: you may discover that they simply like the sound of the school dinners.

## WHEN THERE IS CONFLICT ... WHO MAKES THE FINAL DECISION?

The answer is simple: you do. Your child should of course contribute an opinion, and you should try your best to make sure that your child's opinion and your own are in alignment. Should they differ, however, it is you who is responsible for the decision and all its consequences.

# SHOULD WE START INDEPENDENT SCHOOL THIS EARLY?

When your child is so far away from public exams, is there any point starting independent school at pre-prep or prep?

Nursery children at L'Ecole des Petits

Many parents may feel it makes financial sense to educate their child in the state sector at primary level, and then move them to an independent senior school. Every year, many children across the UK make this transition very happily (see p. 16). However, there are some reasons you might like to consider an independent school at pre-prep and/or prep level.

Even at the lower levels, many independent schools in the UK offer an exceptional standard of schooling, with teaching, facilities and pastoral care that is excellent. You can expect teachers to be dedicated, well-trained, caring and focused; you can expect facilities to be up-to-date and well-maintained, and resources to engage and challenge your child. The class sizes are generally smaller than at state primaries, meaning children benefit from a higher level of personal attention.

## Getting a head start
Independent pre-preps and preps may be an important step, not merely in themselves, but as a stepping stone into the next stage of schooling. If your child is at an all-through school at prep level, you may be able to dispense with the difficulty and stress of the exams at 11+ or 13+—if your child is required to sit these exams at all, they will sit them as an internal candidate. The pressure on junior school places, particularly in London, is filtering down to the nursery sector, some of which are cultivating success in placing their pupils in the all-through schools. Latest reports are that in the capital, mothers-to-be who have not yet given birth are being told that they have already left it too late to secure a place in the top nurseries for their future two-year-olds.

The schools are keen to stress that gaining a place at a school's nursery or pre-prep does not guarantee a place at prep school; just as in the passage from prep to senior school, children who do not make adequate progress are often quietly encouraged to apply to other schools.

However, a school will try to accommodate a child coming with a strong recommendation from the school's own lower years teachers, and so internal candidates have a greater chance of success. ∎

"Educating our children in the independent sector has been the most valuable investment we could have made. It has meant that from the start, our children have had a first rate education with superb, nurturing and inspiring teachers. I think a private education can help with giving a student the extra confidence to 'give it a go' in today's very competitive world."

**KATE,** MOTHER OF TWO DAUGHTERS NOW AT UNIVERSITY, AND A 15-YEAR-OLD SON

Lion House
Pre-Prep
School

# WHAT IS INVOLVED IN
# PRE-PREP AND
# PREP SCHOOL ENTRY?

**Pre-prep and prep school entry varies depending on whether your child is entering at 4+, 7+ or 11+.**

If you are considering an independent school for your child's pre-prep or prep education, you need to know what is involved in the entry process. Rather than applying through your local authority, as in the state sector, you will need to apply directly to the schools themselves. In some cases it will be on the basis of first come, first served; in others your child may have to pass certain academic criteria, or face an interview process.

## Entry at 4+ and below

Entrance to nursery school and pre-prep is usually by date of registration. Several heavily-oversubscribed London schools run a ballot for places at 4+. There may nevertheless be informal processes of selection, even at nursery. Children may be invited to the school for trial sessions, primarily intended to establish that the child does not have an evident learning or social difficulty which the school is not properly equipped to handle. An informal assessment session may be augmented by an interview with parents, typically by the Head, who will want to establish that the school can work cooperatively with the parents in the best interests of the child. At the earliest years, schools may offer a 'settling in' period for the first few months; if a child is not finding their feet, perhaps because they are too young, there may be options for settling in gradually.

## Entry at 7+

Those entering a prep school at this age should register at their preferred independent school as early as possible. While the school may not select children based on date of registration, it still pays to show your interest in a selective school by registering early. The deadline for registrations may be up to a year ahead of the date of entry, usually around October of the previous year. 7+ exams and assessment days are held towards the end of the calendar year preceding entry—that is, in Year 2.

By the age of 7+, children will usually be examined in a more or less formal way. There is a good deal of movement into

"Don't put your child through it unless they are ready and mature enough. At 4+, they mustn't be too shy or the experience will be stressful. At 7+, they need to be bright, and may need to be happy working with a tutor."

**ARABELLA**, PARENT AND MATHS TEACHER

the independent sector at this age: many parents postpone their move to a fee-paying school by using a local state school. When these children do seek entry, the schools will want to know that the child has reached certain educational milestones and will set formal tests. For those applying to a boarding school, 7+ entry will involve an extra round of interviews with Housemasters and mistresses, who will be attempting to recruit a mixture of children who will work well together, to make their house a success. Parents invited to these interviews should be attentive and respectful towards the staff. On no account appear to be in any way pushy, demanding or superior. Co-operative parents are crucial to the success of the child in a school.

## Entry at 11+

A number of students leave their prep schools at the end of Year 6 to enter their senior schools, creating vacancies which the prep schools will be keen to fill. (Note that, because many girls' schools have their major intakes at 11+, the higher years of some prep schools have a major gender imbalance. If you are planning to place your daughter in a prep school to prepare her for 13+ exams, make sure to find a school where there are other girls in the same position.)

The procedures for entry into prep schools at 11+ may be more or less formal, depending on the competitiveness of the school and on how keen they are to fill their vacancies. In order to attract the most able children, the senior schools with attached preps sometimes offer a guaranteed place in the senior school

The Godolphin School, Salisbury

at 13+ for pupils who enter the attached prep school at 11+. In these attached preps, the exams will resemble other 11+ senior school entry exams, because that is in effect what they are. In the stand-alone preps, the testing will usually be less comprehensive and may merely involve the standard CAT tests (**see p. 73**) used for testing potential.

The most important issue at 11+, as far as the prep schools are concerned, is that they will be able to place a child in an appropriate senior school at 13+. Their confidence in this will depend on their assessment of a child's abilities, but also on their assessment of the parent's willingness to take advice. Many parents register their children for 13+ before Year 7, and there is an increasing tendency for senior schools to pre-test children in Year 7 at the very latest. (Registrations to some senior schools may already be closed, though they may consider a late applicant at the behest of a prep school Head.) The prep school Head will want to be confident that they can work with parents toward a successful 13+ placement. If, at this late stage, the parents appear to have circumscribed or unrealistic expectations about potential senior schools for their child, the Head may decide that taking the child on is simply more trouble than it is worth. ■

Middle School pupils at Sevenoaks School. Photo: Jonathan Cole

"We moved our younger daughter from one prep school to another at the age of 11. Changing schools at 11 is not always easy, as the friendship groups are established, and we did worry. However, it turned out to be the right decision, and despite a few wobbles, she settled in quickly and thrived."

**JAMES**, FATHER OF DAUGHTER NOW IN HER 20s

# Parenting

One of the more difficult of a parent's duties is to send a child off to school for their first days. There may be little you can do to make the experience easier for yourself, but you can prepare your child.

moodboard/THINKSTOCK

## WAYS TO PREPARE

• Get into the school routine before term starts. Practise putting on school uniform so that your child can do it easily themselves. Make sure that your child is capable of using a knife and fork, holding a pencil properly and so on. Try to meet with the new teacher.

• Read a book on the subject of starting school, such as Lauren Child's *I Am Too Absolutely Small for School*; or Shirley Hughes' *Lucy and Tom Go to School*.

• Encourage your child to stage a play or compose a story, rehearsing the experience of their first school day. This may allow them to explore their feeling.

• Find a friend starting at the same time, so that they can share their feelings. If this isn't possible, perhaps your child can take along a teddy or doll so as not to feel quite so alone. Reassure them that you will be with them in your thoughts.

### LEARNING ABOUT CHANGE

Change can mean new friends, and new things to do; it can also mean not knowing what to be or do. Go through the pros and cons of change with your child.

### ASK YOURSELF...

Will I be upset about my child starting school? Will it upset my child, if they realise I am upset?

### ASK YOUR CHILD...

Is anything worrying you about starting school?

### TALKING TO YOUR CHILD ABOUT SCHOOL

Do not expect too much of your child. On the first few days, it is enough if your child can report a single thing that went well. Report what you did with your day, in the hope that your child will do the same—and also to give them a way of imagining you when they are away from you. Expect your child to be tired out by their day and adjust your family rituals to allow for more rest.

### WHAT IF THE SCHOOL IS GOOD, BUT MY CHILD ISN'T HAPPY?

In recent years, the educational climate has become increasingly focused on results and measurable outcomes. However, as a happy child is a more confident learner, it is important you choose a school that fits your child's personality. If your child is not happy, and you have exhausted all possibilities for improving their experience, consider moving schools—no matter how good its outcomes may be.

### HOW WILL I KNOW IF MY CHILD IS HAPPY?

A parent's inclination is to watch for signs that things are not going well. It is reasonable to assume that, if your child is not happy, it should not take long for this to become fully apparent. Some educationalists suggest, however, that it is wise to set the bar higher: assume that it should be fully apparent if your child is happy. If it is not clear that things are actively going well, then there may be something that you or the school can do to rectify the situation.

moodboard/THINKSTOCK

# WHAT WILL THE ASSESSMENT BE LIKE?

Pre-prep and prep admissions are not as standardised as 11+ or 13+ admissions, so each school will have to tell you their own procedure.

"At 7+, we assess girls in:

- Reading a simple story fluently and giving a clear oral account of the points within it.
- Structuring and developing a piece of writing in narrative form and showing good spelling.
- Demonstrating a knowledge of the meaning of numbers through experience in using them, for example counting or grouping different objects or scoring in games.
- Their knowledge of multiplication tables.
- Demonstrating experience of different coins, perhaps by playing shopping games.
- Showing experience of time, measurement, length, weight and capacity.

The exam is the first of several assessment sessions. If successful in the exams, you may proceed to an interview, and finally to a practical assessment. In these practical sessions, girls are assessed in:

- Interaction with other pupils and staff.
- Experience of scientific inquiry through contexts taken from life processes, materials and their physical properties.
- Displaying an inquisitive mind and an interest in finding out why and how things happen.
- Interest in visits and trips they have made and creative activities such as painting, using construction toys, cooking, sewing or making scrapbooks."

**CITY OF LONDON GIRLS' SCHOOL WEBSITE**

## 4+

There is no standard form of assessment of children at this early age; each school will have its own approach. The one constant is that assessments at this age are practical in nature.

The tasks your child will perform are play-based; they are designed to be fun. The school will be testing a range of skills: linguistic, numerical, perceptual, interpersonal and social.

A child will not normally be expected to be reading or writing at this age, but may be asked to listen to a story and answer questions about it, to paint a picture, solve a puzzle, cut out a shape or build something out of construction materials.

Assessments commonly last about an hour. For schools which have many applicants at an early age, assessment of the children may be conducted in a group situation, with others of the same age.

## 7+

Many schools have selective entry at 7+ and so conduct competitive entry exams. These tests are typically in English and Mathematics, and a general Reasoning test is also often included. Different schools conduct their admissions processes in their own ways, but the standard format is a two-stage process, including a combined exam in these subjects, whereupon children are selected for interview. Some schools interview all children at the same time as the exam. Children will be interviewed by a senior staff member, either individually or in a group situation. Interviews conducted as a group often involve a problem-solving task of some form, designed to test a child's listening skills, their intellectual curiosity, their problem-solving skills and their ability to work collaboratively. Children may also be interviewed individually, to identify individual talents or aptitudes that may be of particular interest to the school.

## 11+

In preps attached to senior schools, admissions at 11+ will typically involve a set of formal exams taken at the prep school in English, Mathematics and Reasoning, and sometimes a general Science paper as well.

In stand-alone preps, testing at 11+ may be less comprehensive. Prep schools commonly assess a child's potential by conducting CAT tests (**see p. 73.**) ∎

# HOW SHOULD MY CHILD
# PREPARE
## FOR PRE-PREP AND
## PREP ADMISSIONS?

gpointstudio/iSTOCK/THINKSTOCK

**Preparation at this age is less about revision and more about encouraging confidence and a willingness to learn.**

Before deciding on your preparation programme for the prep school admissions test, make sure that you scour the school's website for information about what the school is looking for. Some schools produce leaflets outlining the specific admissions criteria at the various entrance levels. These may be available on the school's website or may be sent to you once you make a registration. You should tailor your preparation to the criteria outlined. If there is no information available on admissions criteria, ask the Registrar for further information. Broadly speaking, at these lower levels the schools are looking for evidence of potential, whereas at the higher educational levels, the schools are looking for evidence of ability or achievement.

## 4+

No particular preparation is required for admissions at the earliest ages. The best preparation is simply to talk to your child, to read to them and to play games that encourage intellectual curiosity. At the earliest entrance levels, the schools will be looking for evidence of parental involvement in their children's education. They are looking for children who will be supported in their home environments to achieve their best. This will express itself, not in the ability to perform a particular list of tasks, but in something deeper: a willingness to persevere, so as to discover how things work and why things happen the way they do. They are looking, in other words, for potential.

## 7+

By 7+, the schools are more explicit about what they are looking for in the children they select than at younger stages. It is debatable whether at this stage you need to buy workbooks or to become familiar with the Key Stage 1 curriculum. The prep schools are more interested in potential than achievement, and a good school will be confident of filling any gaps there may be in your child's education, so it is better to encourage your child to develop their own interests and talents than to try to tick the various boxes of achievement at this age. However, it would still be wise to ensure that your child knows how to perform the standard skills expected of a child of this age: to add the coins needed to pay for an ice cream, to tell the time sufficiently to work out when a cake will be cooked, to spell the most common 500 words and so on. For schools which do conduct formal exams in English, Mathematics and Reasoning, you can find materials in the education section of your local bookshop or online. WHSmith produce a range of books at this level, as do Bonds,

imtmphoto/iSTOCK/THINKSTOCK

CGP, Letts, Schofield and Sims and others. The differences between the books produced by these publishers at this level is not so great as to be of huge importance. It is perhaps better to choose books that look appealing to your child, in the hope that they will make it through to the end of them.

## 11+

For 11+ entry into prep schools with attached senior schools, your preparation should resemble the preparation of other 11+ applicants, since such applications more closely resemble other senior school admissions than prep school admissions.

(There is a range of materials suggested for 11+ preparation on p. 85).

The stand-alone prep schools are typically more flexible in their admissions at 11+; some of these schools will be attempting to fill places vacated by the students who have left for their senior schools and so will be pleased to find a place for your child.

The most common form of testing at this level is by CAT testing. (See p. 73 for more on CAT tests.)

In theory, no preparation is needed for these tests, but it is wise to give your child some practice in Reasoning skills, by way of books of Verbal and Non-verbal

Reasoning available online or from the educational section of the local bookshop. Besides solid marks in these tests, the prep school will be looking for intellectual curiosity and an eagerness for learning in your child's interview. So some practice of presentation at interview is also advised. ■

The Parent Brief's Aiming High can teach you invaluable tricks for encouraging impressive critical thinking in young children

### HERE TO HELP

"Should children be prepped for 7+ school admissions? Good heavens, no. Education is about human flourishing. Prepping for 7+ exams reduces that noble aim to a narrow rat-race for results—and too much of that already follows in later years. Any school or parent endorsing such an approach has lost sight of what education for young children is about. Taken to extremes, such an approach is responsible for the breakdown in mental health of our young people today. Schools and parents will undoubtedly claim pressure of numbers on a finite number of places. Nevertheless, the best schools will adjust their admissions procedures to be broad-minded, subjective and human, not simply driven by 'results'."

**BEN THOMAS, HEADMASTER OF THOMAS'S, BATTERSEA**

# HOW CAN I HELP? ON THE DAY

**Bringing your child to their first assessment day can be an emotional moment for you, but there are ways to make it less stressful for your child.**

At this early age, it's wise to try to keep the testing or interview day as relaxed as possible, so do not make too much fuss about it. Your child should be neatly dressed, but you should not need to buy special clothes to wear. If your child is already at a school with a uniform, then it is easiest and best to wear this uniform to all testing and interview sessions. Younger children not yet at school should simply wear something comfortable and presentable. If you are applying for a place at a prep school at 11+, you might consider a shirt and blazer for your son, but a tie is not necessary.

The letter confirming the time and date of the testing/interview will inform you of anything particular you should bring on the day. Apart from this, the school will provide anything needed. Schools sometimes ask children to bring something that is special to them, just to get the interview off the ground. It does not matter too much what this is, so long as your child has something to say about it. An object with a personal significance to them—something they have made, an object from their childhood or photos— would be perfect. ■

## STRAIGHT FROM THE HORSE'S MOUTH

"Most schools will send information in advance about what to expect on the day of an assessment. In broad terms, my advice would be to treat the event in as 'low key' a way as possible: you want your child to feel relaxed and comfortable, not wound-up and anxious. Therefore, stick to the normal routine: if it is a school day, your child should wear school uniform; whoever normally takes the child to school should take them to the assessment, and so on. If you are calm and happy (or at least appear so!), your child will be too."

**BEN THOMAS**, HEADMASTER OF THOMAS'S, BATTERSEA

# Parenting

When making decisions about independent education at this young age, one thing that is bound to factor highly is how your child will respond to the admissions process. Young children react very differently to stressful situations: some may find it unsettling, but others may sail blithely through the process, enjoying the added attention.

monkeybusinessimages/iSTOCK/THINKSTOCK

## WHAT MIGHT YOUR CHILD BE WORRYING ABOUT?

- Some children may realise that you are attaching importance to these admissions and be stressed by that.
- Your child may worry about not getting into the same school as their friends.
- If your child hasn't sat tests or exams before, this can be daunting.

## ASK YOURSELF...

Are you managing the way your wishes and hopes are expressed? Especially at the youngest ages, your child's worries are likely to centre around pleasing you rather than their own preferences for schools.

## PREPARING FOR DISAPPOINTMENT

If you are applying for an oversubscribed school, alert your child to the fact that such schools have certain admissions criteria. Particularly if your child's friends are also applying, you may need to explain that they and their friends may just be suited to different schools. On the other hand, to avoid adding extra stress, you may find it better simply to leave the question to fate, and deal with the disappointment later should it arise.

## TALKING TO YOUR CHILD ABOUT FAILURE

At this early stage of education, there are no passes or fails. If your child does not gain entry to your chosen school now, there will be other opportunities; you and your child should simply regroup and try again later. In the meantime, there are other schools where they will be just as happy. Learning this calm approach to getting results now will help at later, more competitive stages.

## DOES YOUR CHILD NEED A HEALTHY AMOUNT OF STRESS?

Some children seemingly fail to appreciate that there should be stress attached to this situation at all. If you have such a child, you may be worried that they will not try hard enough if they do not realise the importance. However, the best advice is to do nothing to rock the boat. These may be the children who are most likely to succeed in the admissions process, because they are the most likely to present themselves just as they are.

# WHEN SHOULD MY CHILD CHANGE SCHOOLS?

In many cases, your chosen senior school will dictate at what age your child will transfer—but where you have the choice, there are a few factors you might like to consider.

In the independent school sector in the UK, senior school can begin at either 11+ or 13+; the 11+ exams are taken for entry into Year 7, and the 13+ exams are taken for entry into Year 9. Children generally take one set of exams or the other. A few children may take both, if they enter an 11+ school and then elect to move on to a 13+ school two years later, but this is uncommon.

Which exams your child sits depends on whether your chosen school has its major

> "I moved my daughter at 11+ as she needed an environment in which she could be stretched. Senior school could provide her the challenges she needed."
> **SHAREEN,** PARENT

intake at 11+ or at 13+. As a general rule, the schools with an intake at Year 7 are the girls' schools and the co-educational schools which, having been established more recently than the old 'public' schools, have adapted to the fact that primary schools finish at Year 6. Those with their first intake at Year 9 tend to be established boys' schools which assume that children attend prep schools, which traditionally continue to Year 8. Some schools have entry points at both levels. In that case, you should establish the relative availability of places and work out which is the best entry point for you.

When your child changes schools will also depend on the type of school your child is coming from. Many prep schools continue to Year 8, to accommodate children sitting the 13+ exams—but some finish at Year 6, meaning

that the pupils must either transfer to their senior schools at 11+ or transfer to another prep school for Years 7 and 8, before moving on to their senior schools at 13+. Children coming from state primary schools which finish at Year 6 are in the same situation.

## Moving from a state primary

If your child attends a state primary school and you wish to transfer to an independent school with a 13+ entry, you will need to decide when it is best to move into the independent sector, considering the options available to you. Many schools with 13+ entry use the Common Entrance exams as the basis of their admissions procedures. In order to pass these exams, your child must be at a school which prepares children for them: that is why they are called 'prep' schools. The Common Entrance

# AUTHOR'S TIPS

## 6 THINGS TO CONSIDER WHEN **CHOOSING** WHEN TO **CHANGE SCHOOLS**

**1** If the school is selective, establish the relative **availability of places** and at which level you have the best chance of gaining admission.

**2** Look at when your child's **peers** are changing schools. This is particularly an issue for girls, for whom the 11+ entry point is more common: you don't want your daughter to find herself the only girl left in her class, her friends having all moved on.

**3** Consider the **maturity** of your child, both intellectually and emotionally.

**4** Evaluate the **quality of the prep school** they attend. If your child attends a prep school where they are happy and flourishing, and does not seem ready to move on to a larger and more impersonal senior school, it may be better to keep your child where they are until the end of Year 8.

**5** Children with SEN may benefit from having longer to work on their learning difficulties before sitting the senior school entrance exams. On the other hand, the senior school may have more specialised **SEN provision**.

**6** Bear in mind that the **Common Entrance course** offered by prep schools in Years 7 and 8 is particularly good. Not only does it produce high standards in its Year 8 Common Entrance candidates, it is also very good practice for the GCSE exams taken three years later.

*George Doyle/STOCKBYTE/THINKSTOCK*

programme takes two years, starting in Year 7. Thus primary children typically make the move into the independent sector at the beginning of Year 7. Some prep school Heads argue, however, that the move is best made earlier, at Year 5 or Year 6 at the latest, to give the child a better chance to prepare themselves for the intensive demands of the Common Entrance programme. A number of prep schools thus

**Pupil at Falcons Boys' School**

have a 10+ entry. The children who move at 10+ may find the transition from state primary school to independent senior school to be smoother. The junior schools attached to independent seniors sometimes have entry points at 10+, for the same purpose. Less commonly, these schools may also conduct an 11+ deferred entry: a set of exams, similar in form to the 11+, which a child sits at 10+ to secure a place in Year 7. These may be intended to attract the brightest state school children prior to their application for grammar schools. **(see p. 16 for more on moving from the state sector).**

### Delaying a year

When the registrations for each year group open, the schools will specify the dates between which applicants must be born: typically September 1 of one year and August 31 of the following. In this way, a year group will be strictly uniform in age. If you have a child whom you believe would benefit from being placed a year ahead or a year below their peers, discuss this with the Registrar or Head of prospective schools. Children who are born in July and August can sometimes be disadvantaged in these exams—even though,

*PURESTOCK/THINKSTOCK*

recognising this fact, schools tend to make provision for them. A school may consider deferring entry for a year, if it appears that the child is not yet intellectually or emotionally ready to move on to their senior school. ■

"I decided to keep my daughter at her prep school at 11. She was happy and settled; I do not want to disrupt her life unless it's absolutely necessary."
**LAURA, WHOSE DAUGHTER ATTENDS A KENT CO-ED**

# WHAT
## IS THE PROCESS FOR
# 13+ ENTRY?

**While individual schools will have their own procedures, there are two main paths to 13+ entry that your child might follow.**

**13+** entry is an entirely different process from 11+ entry, and indeed, the process can vary depending on the school to which you are applying. It is important, therefore, to look into the specific processes of the schools in which you are interested.

The 13+ admissions process is generally a more protracted affair than the 11+; in most schools, the process will take several years to complete. Most children register for two or three schools; you will save yourself time and effort if you enrol for one school only, but this course of action is usually only advised where child and school are clearly very well-matched. Applications at 13+ tend to be more closely targeted to the child's academic abilities than at 11+, and the prep

school Heads tend to take a more active role in guiding their pupils towards schools that are at the right level.

The distinction between 11+ and 13+ is important: some schools have an intake at

> ## The 13+ admissions process is generally a more protracted affair than the 11+; in most schools, the process will take several years

both 11+ and 13+, and some 13+ schools have a junior school attached with its own intake at 11+. For those who wish to enter the senior school at 13+, entry into an attached junior school at 11+ is an excellent option; children

who are accepted into the junior school often proceed without hitch directly into the senior school. The junior school will prepare its pupils specifically for the exams—and in particular, for the scholarship exams—of the senior school. The senior school may in turn give preference to candidates from its junior school and may even reserve places specifically for these children.

### What is Common Entrance?

The Common Entrance exams are taken by the majority of independent school applicants at 13+. They are so-called because they are common to all the schools that use them, as opposed to exams set by the schools themselves (which confusingly, are often referred to as Common Entrance, even

# 8 STEPS TO **13+ ENTRY**

**1** **School visits.** The 13+ process starts with visits to prospective schools in Years 4, 5 or 6. These visits may be on open days or school tours taken individually or in groups. They often include a talk by the Head, demonstrations in the classrooms, a tour by a pupil and various other activities or performances.

**2** **Registration.** Depending on the school, registration can take place from Year 5 to Year 7. Some schools have a window for registrations, while others have a strict deadline. Registration for a school usually costs around £100 (but may be higher) and the fee is non-refundable once paid.

**3** **References.** All schools require a reference from the child's present school, which asks about present levels of attainment and projections for coming years. The reference is confidential: you cannot expect to have input into it or see what it contains. This reference may be lengthy, and require the input of both the prep school Head and form teacher.

**4** **Pre-tests.** Some schools use pre-tests (see p. 73) to filter out the applicants who will sit formal exams at 13+. They usually take place in Year 6 or 7, and consist of exams in English, Mathematics and Reasoning, or may take the form of an online Cognitive Ability Test (CAT).

**5** **Interviews.** Interviews usually take place in Year 6 or 7, though they may take place in Year 8. In some schools, interviews precede the pre-test; in others, the order is reversed. These interviews are usually conducted in the senior school by the Head or a senior member of staff; some schools also require interviews with the housemaster or mistress of an applicant's prospective house.

**6** **Conditional offers.** If, as a result of their pre-tests, your child is considering more than one Common Entrance school, you need to decide by the beginning of March of the year of the Common Entrance exams, when the prep school enrols the child's name and prospective school with ISEB. In reality, however, the decision will be wanted earlier.

**7** **Exams.** The exams take place in Year 8—that is, the year preceding entry. Common Entrance exams take up one intensive week in June; school-set exams are conducted during January or February. The subjects taken will vary; schools that set their own exams should provide details of the syllabus upon registration.

**8** **Final results.** The results of the school-set exams should be received by March, when registration for Common Entrance is required. The children who accept offers at these schools no longer need to sit Common Entrance exams. The results of the Common Entrance exams are typically sent through to the Head of the child's prep school by the end of the week following the exams. If the child has achieved the required grades, parents will receive a final offer to enrol at the school and pay a deposit.

though this term does not technically apply).

Common Entrance exams are set by the Independent Schools Examinations Board (ISEB), a group of prep and senior school teachers, who also write the syllabus for the two-year programme. ('Common Entrance' is also another name for the two-year period of study and for the syllabus itself.)

The Common Entrance exams differ from other 11+ and 13+ exams in several respects.

One major difference is that the Common Entrance exams are taken for one school only, the 'right' to sit the exam for that school having been established in advance usually by pre-testing, or discussion between the prep and senior schools. In the two years preceding the Common Entrance exams, the range of schools for which one is seeking admission is whittled down to a single school. Each school specifies a minimum qualifying

mark for success in the Common Entrance exam, which they consider achievable by the children to whom they have made conditional offers. This means that, unlike 11+ and school-set 13+ exams, the Common Entrance exams are qualifying, rather than competitive.

Applicants sit these exams in a wider range of subjects than they typically do for school-set exams: while most 13+ applicants can expect to sit English, Mathematics, one or ▶

more of the Sciences, and a modern European language, Common Entrance applicants also sit History, Geography, Religious Education, and Latin (which, while optional, is required by most selective schools). There are different levels that can be taken in several of these subjects; the senior school stipulates the level it requires of its prospective students.

A final difference is that the exams normally take place at the child's own prep school, which sends the papers to each child's chosen senior school to be marked. The prep school administers the process as well, registering the child for the exams (although it is the parents' responsibility first to register their child at their chosen school) and receiving the results, which are then passed on to parents and to the child. By contrast, the school-set exams take place at the senior school for which your child is applying.

## Will my child take Common Entrance?

In theory, the two paths diverge during the course of Years 7 and 8. If a child sits pre-tests for a school which uses the Common Entrance exams, and then accepts a conditional offer at that school, then they will sit Common Entrance exams for admission. If a child sits exams set by an independent senior school that does not use Common Entrance exams, and then proceeds to accept an offer of a place at that school, then they will not need to sit Common Entrance exams. However, a child may register for a school that uses Common Entrance and also for schools that use their own exams and so pursue both paths at the same time. A school may even use different forms of exam for different applicants: Common Entrance for those coming from a prep school and school-set exams for those who do not.

luckat/ISTOCK/THINKSTOCK

## MORE ON COMMON ENTRANCE—FROM THE MAN WHO RUNS IT

"ISEB has been providing Common Entrance exams for entry into independent senior schools for over 100 years. These examinations are not weighed down by tradition, however: they are bang up to date. They are academically rigorous assessments, demanding high standards across a wide range of subjects. Prep schools are using our 11+ exams as part of their ongoing academic tracking and assessment of pupils who will take their Common Entrance at 13+. As more and more senior schools decide to pre-test their candidates one or two years prior to Common Entrance, ISEB now offers the very popular online, adaptive, age-standardised Common Pre-Tests, which prep school pupils can sit in their own prep schools. These are tests designed with the best interests of the pupils in mind and are proving highly successful.

Common Entrance at 13+ is aligned with the National Curriculum. ISEB provides schools with comprehensive syllabuses and a framework for learning. Great emphasis is placed on testing skills, as well as subject knowledge and understanding. Common Entrance at 13+ thus encourages candidates to study in depth across a broad range of subjects, but at a level appropriate to their ability. There are lots of opportunities for critical thinking, problem solving and independent learning.

For very good reasons, Common Entrance is widely regarded as the 'gold standard' in the independent school world: some 220 senior schools participate, including the country's most famous and successful institutions, as well as over 400 prep schools in the UK and in 50 countries around the world."

**PETER KIRK,** CHAIRMAN, INDEPENDENT SCHOOLS EXAMINATIONS BOARD (ISEB)

## Entrance to boarding schools

Boarding schools typically conduct a more extensive interview and activity programme for preselection to their schools. Applicants will be invited to the school overnight or over a weekend, where academic exams and interviews are conducted, along with a programme of team activities and events requiring the child's participation. The aim is two-fold: to give the child a taste of boarding life at the school, so that they can determine whether it is right for them, and to give the school a broader picture of the child's abilities. These may be conducted at any stage, but often around a year prior to entry.

## Scholarship applicants

At 13+, scholarship applicants to Common Entrance schools are treated separately, normally taking exams set by the schools themselves. In this respect, they are treated more like candidates on the non-Common Entrance path; they will not sit their exams at their prep school, for example, but at the schools themselves. Scholarship Exam applicants who do not win a scholarship are still considered for entry, and are not disadvantaged against those who take the Common Entrance exams.

**(For more on scholarships, see p. 63.)** ■

# HOW DIFFICULT
## IS THE ADMISSIONS PROCESS ?

**The difficulty of the admissions process is largely dependent on the school, and in particular, how many children apply.**

Girls at King's School, Canterbury

For many independent senior schools, especially those outside the main urban centres, entry is relatively straightforward. Provided that your child is willing to work to their potential, such a school will be pleased to receive your application. The 11+ or 13+ entrance exams will simply show that your child has achieved satisfactory progress in their schooling to date. While applicants should try to present themselves at their best, the exams should not be particularly stressful because they will not be particularly competitive.

Many schools, however, receive more applications than they have capacity for. These schools are 'oversubscribed'. Oversubscription is a particular problem at 11+ and 13+, when many children in the independent sector move between prep schools and their chosen senior schools. This is also a point at which many children enter the independent sector from primary schools and from overseas, increasing the competition for the available places.

In the most oversubscribed schools, there may be around ten applicants for every place. These schools—called 'selective schools' or 'superselectives'—select the applicants they consider most likely to flourish in their schools.

The most obvious effect of oversubscription is that a school's admissions exams will be more competitive. If you are applying to oversubscribed schools, you will need to give thought to your child's strengths, so that they can be presented in the best possible light. You also need to ensure they are at a reasonable academic level for the exams, and prepare them for the other aspects of the admissions process as well: the interview, in particular. Oversubscription also means you may need to register for more than one school. Many parents—particularly at 11+—register at numerous schools, which further exacerbates the problem of oversubscription.

That said, it is also important not to be put off by the numbers of children applying to a given school, because on average those children will have applied to three or four schools—and some to many more. There is at present a place for every child who applies for one in the UK independent sector. The reality is that the vast majority of children receive offers from more than one school and the vast majority are fully satisfied with the offer they finally accept. ∎

## IN THE KNOW

Two types of school are particularly affected by oversubscription: the most prestigious of the old 'public' schools, which are increasingly attracting international applicants, and the London day schools.

# HOW MANY SCHOOLS SHOULD WE APPLY TO?

The question about how many schools to apply to depends to an extent on the competition for places at the school.

London schools are especially popular.
Photo: Finton House Prep

I f you are applying to schools which are not oversubscribed, being accepted by the school is relatively straightforward. You follow the school's admissions process:

> "I'd say three is an optimum number of schools to apply to—and definitely no more than five."
>
> **SUSAN,** PARENT OF 11-YEAR-OLD DAUGHTER AT A LONDON DAY SCHOOL

your child will generally sit an exam, present references from their present school and come to an interview. Provided they are working at a satisfactory level, gaining entry to the school should not be a problem. In those circumstances you need not apply to more than one school. If you are unsure whether the school that interests you is oversubscribed, simply ask the Registrar whether there is competition for places.

If you are applying to schools that are oversubscribed, however, this will likely ▶

**STRAIGHT FROM THE HORSE'S MOUTH**

> "We have a strong and stated sibling, alumnae and early registration policy, so these girls are considered first. For all girls, we look at their entrance exam, their prep or primary school report, any special talents and their interview here at school."
>
> **MARY BREEN,** HEAD OF ST MARY'S SCHOOL ASCOT

A large choir at Canford School

influence how many and which schools you apply to. In this situation many parents apply to schools of varying academic selectivity: one where it will be difficult for their child to get in; one school where it is reasonable to expect their child to gain admission; and one school where they fully expect their child to be accepted.

There is some luck involved in any school application: your child may be in absolutely tip-top form during an exam or interview and so receive an offer that is unexpected. But as a general rule, if you do not gain admission to one highly selective school, you will probably not gain admission into another at the same level of selectivity. This, then, is the first rule of admissions to independent senior schools in the UK: give yourself back-up. If your child is not strong academically, do not waste time, energy and money applying to a number of schools that are highly academically selective. Aside from anything else, consider how many exams it is reasonable to ask your child to sit.

## Academic selection

Note that the academic selectivity of a school in its admissions is separate from the priority the school gives to academic achievement. A school will be oversubscribed because many parents want their children to go to it, but the reason why these parents want their children to go to that school may not be that it is the most academic of schools. It may be that it is highly prestigious, for example. It may even be popular because it is not so very academic. Nevertheless, because the school is oversubscribed, it can select those with the best results in its exams. ■

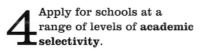

AUTHOR'S TIPS

# 10 TIPS FOR REGISTERING FOR
## OVERSUBSCRIBED SCHOOLS

**1** **Do not apply to too many schools; three or four is plenty. Too many means that you will overburden your child with exams and interviews.**

**2** If one school is more important to you than others, try to ensure that it is not the **first exam** your child sits. (The schools publish exam dates well in advance.) The first exam is usually the most taxing, psychologically; your child could sit an exam for a school that was not originally on your list, simply for the practice.

**3** Consider the **intake of the schools** to which you are applying. If each of the schools that interest you has limited availability, add a school to your list with a larger intake. Note: if a school is co-educational, only half of their intake is available to you.

**4** Apply for schools at a range of levels of **academic selectivity**.

**5** **Do not be put off** by the numbers applying to oversubscribed schools. Some parents apply to a vast number of schools, which dramatically inflates the number of candidates for the various schools.

**6** **Consider adding a school to your list where you are not confident of success. Your child may surprise you.**

**7** But remember, gaining admission to a school that is **too academic** for your child does no-one a favour in the long run. Being rejected is demoralising, but nothing compared to the demoralising effect of languishing at the bottom of the class.

**8** **Give yourself backup,** for your own peace of mind. Find a school where you are confident of success, and that would serve, if your child were not accepted at the other schools you have registered for.

**9** Ask if a school has a policy of **prioritising siblings**; it may save trouble when it comes to your younger children.

**10** Try not to let yourself be influenced too heavily by what others are doing. Have confidence in your own impressions of which school is right for your child; **you know your child best**.

# SHOULD MY CHILD AIM FOR A SCHOLARSHIP?

If you are considering applying for a scholarship, establish exactly what the school's procedures are for the assessment of scholarship applicants.

Papplewick School's scholars

## THE DIFFERENCE BETWEEN 13+ COMMON ENTRANCE AND SCHOLARSHIP EXAMS

"The scholarship route is more challenging than Common Entrance. The exams are more difficult, but also more stimulating—good for extending the clever children. My son's scholarship class was small; it was conducted rather like a tutorial group. He spent his days working together with the brightest of the kids in his year and he enjoyed the stimulation of working at the higher level. As for the advantages of being a scholar: there is a financial advantage, but there is also the honour of calling yourself a scholar, which the boys appreciate. As it happened, my son missed out on a scholarship. It was worthwhile nonetheless, because the course leading up to the exams was so good academically."

**ANDREA**, WHOSE SON SAT THE SCHOLARSHIP EXAM FOR A LONDON BOYS' SCHOOL

At 11+, applicants are often automatically enrolled for a school's scholarships, which are offered to those who perform most impressively in the exams and interviews. The same is true of some schools that conduct their own exams at 13+. Many schools, however—and especially those that use 13+ Common Entrance exams—consider scholarship applicants separately from other students, assessing them by way of specific scholarship exams set by the school. To complicate matters further, ISEB offers scholarship papers as well as the standard Common Entrance papers at 13+, which a number of schools have adopted for scholarship applicants; these are called Common Academic Scholarship Exams (CASE).

At 13+, scholarship candidates sit the scholarship exams for the same school as they would otherwise sit Common Entrance. Since the scholarship papers are at a higher level than the Common Entrance papers, the results are taken in place of Common Entrance results. A child who fails to achieve the required level in these exams may sit Common Entrance exams in some or all subjects to rectify their results. The 13+ scholarship exams are conducted over several days at the senior school prior to the Common Entrance exams—usually in April or May of Year 8, but can be as early as January—with results posted a couple of weeks later.

Scholarship exams may include a general paper, with questions on logic, current events and/or ethical issues. They also require a deeper understanding of the subjects examined: the English exam, for example, may set extracts from Keats ▶

Art at Felsted School

## WHAT TO EXPECT ON THE SCHOLARSHIP PAPERS

**Write a short essay in answer to one of the following questions:**

1. Should prisoners be given the right to vote? Justify your view.

2. Should the first-past-the-post system for electing MPs be replaced by Alternative Vote?

3. Do British newspapers add to, or subtract from, democracy in Britain?

4. What do the recent events in Egypt, Bahrain, Tunisia and Libya tell us?

5. How should groups like the English Defence League be opposed?

**Taken from the 13+ Scholarship exam for St Edward's Oxford**

and Dickens, rather than contemporary writers.

If your child does not attend a prep school that prepares children specifically for the scholarship papers, it will be difficult to compete in them. These schools are typically the larger prep schools, which select scholarship children in Year 7 and teach them in a separate scholarship set. A small prep school may not be in a position to prepare your child adequately for Scholarship exams, so if you think this will be an issue, you need to raise the matter well in advance.

## Other forms of scholarship

Those applying for scholarships in art, music, drama and sport can expect to be examined in their chosen field. Applicants for art scholarships must show an impressive portfolio and may also sit a practical exam. Applicants for music scholarships must have attained certain grades in at least two instruments (often, a Distinction at

Grade 6 and Pass at Grade 3). Applicants for drama scholarships may need to present a prepared piece and a series of improvisational exercises. Evidence of public performances in an established orchestra or theatre company will help music and drama applications. So too with sporting scholarships: the schools will want evidence of achievements in public competitions, beyond the A-team in the child's prep school. Many schools receive applications from children in regional and national teams. Lastly, some schools offer all-round scholarships, designed to pick out children with a combination of skills or those who have demonstrated leadership potential in some way. Note that those selected for non-academic scholarships will still need to sit Common Entrance exams or other school-set exams and to reach the stipulated levels.

If you are considering entering your child for a scholarship, be sure to establish what

is expected of scholarship recipients and whether the expectations are acceptable to you. Some scholarships may commit a child to many hours of music or sports training per week—a commitment that may inhibit their access to other activities or impact on their grades. Scholarships at 11+ or even at 13+ may only be offered until Year 11, so take care that this commitment does not compromise their GCSE results and so their chances of a place in Sixth Form. This is particularly important because, as you will soon discover, scholarships may not be particularly lucrative. For both 11+ and 13+ scholarships, a 10% reduction of fees is common. Some scholarships may be up to 50%, but others again are purely nominal: it is the honour of being able to call oneself a 'scholar' or an 'exhibitioner' that is at stake. That said, success in a scholarship may allow your child to be considered for, or increase your child's chances of obtaining, a bursary. ∎

# Parenting

For many parents, the 11+ and 13+ admissions process will be their first experience of feeling that their child's future lies in the hands of others. This will naturally be stressful. The best strategy is to prepare as best you can for those aspects of the admissions process where you can take control. This will at least give you a psychological advantage, in feeling that you are not entirely at the mercy of fate.

RimDream/iSTOCK/THINKSTOCK

## TAKE THE STRESS OFF YOUR CHILD

It's vital at 11+/13+ admissions that you relieve your child of as much stress as you can. This is a balancing act: you need to involve your child in decision-making, but you do not want them to worry about the decisions made. Only you can decide the right balance for your child.

## REMIND YOURSELF OF THE POSITIVES

For all their difficulty, both 11+ and 13+ exams are worthwhile. One of the reasons that independent schools do so well in GCSE results is that their pupils have already experienced a major set of exams. So do not begrudge the time that you will devote to these exams. Your child is learning valuable lessons that will stand them in good stead later on.

## KEEP ANXIETIES TO YOURSELF

At times, in order to get another Verbal Reasoning exercise cracked or list of French vocab learned, many parents will find themselves feigning an optimism that they do not actually feel. This too can be unnerving, but it is important that your child is not burdened with your anxieties.

## WHITE LIES

How much information is good for your child? Perhaps, if your child asks when the results are due, you might tell them a later date to save them the worry that would otherwise plague them in the days prior to the letters' arrival. Any small tricks that can be used to protect your child from worry are surely justified.

## THE LESSONS YOUR CHILD IS LEARNING

There are even more fundamental lessons being learnt here, too: that some things are hard, but are nevertheless worth doing properly; that hard work is the surest route to success; and that there is enjoyment to be had in working hard and succeeding.

## ASK YOUR CHILD...

Where is the pressure coming from: from school, from friends, from home, from you yourself? What would they like you to do to make things easier for them?

## ASK YOUR FRIENDS...

What did they do to make the admissions process easier for their children? Seek advice wherever you can: parents who have been through 11+/13+ admissions are an invaluable source of help.

# HOW SHOULD MY CHILD PREPARE?

**Preparation at 11+ and 13+ is about more than just revision.**

TAGSTOCK1/ISTOCK/THINKSTOCK

In order to prepare for the formal exams at 11+ and 13+, your child will need to revise the material on the curriculum to be sure it is fresh in their mind. They may have to learn vocab and dates, or practise essay technique and mental maths. However, there are many reasons why children might underperform in exams which have very little to do with their academic ability or knowledge. They may be nervous or excited; they may not be used to concentrating for the amount of time required to complete the exam; they may not be sufficiently disciplined in organising their time and therefore may spend too long on one question at the expense of others. These problems commonly arise because children have little experience of formal exams. Therefore, one of the most important aspects of preparation for 11+ and 13+ exams is simply to practise.

## Learning exam technique

Exam technique involves learning to keep a mental list of the things you need to check on as you work: writing your answer neatly in the correct place; transposing your answer correctly from your rough jottings to the answer sheet; adding the correct units in Maths or using the correct punctuation in English. Finally, exam technique involves learning how to assign your time, and give answers which equate to the marks assigned to the question.

There is only one way to learn exam technique effectively: specimen exams, conducted under exam-like conditions, to teach how it is done. Practice papers do not always include marking schemes, but may show the marks allocated for each question, which is useful for teaching your child how to allocate their time in the exam. Don't worry about being too precise in the marking: the mark attained is less important than the practice these papers provide. If you mark these papers together with your child, you will reinforce what they have learnt.

### HERE TO HELP

"Plan early. Set goals early. Get help early. Ask for assistance with understanding and learning immediately, not months later during a cramming 'revision session'. Work hard during your lessons in the term time, and don't think that anyone else should do the learning for you. Be honest and admit when you could simply work harder—it will make a great deal of difference to you in later life. So, work hard at the right times and do loads of practice papers."

**TOM ROGERSON, HEADMASTER OF COTTESMORE SCHOOL**

## A parent's role

If done diligently, exam preparation will probably require as much of your time as your child's: finding the materials to work on, marking, explaining, confidence-building and so on. If you plan to help your child with exam preparation, you will need time in the evenings and at the weekend with your child to do it. You need a space where your child can concentrate on their work without distractions (and if such a space is not available at home, you need to find it somewhere else). You need good organisation to keep track of what has been achieved and what still has to be done;

you need a good supply of work materials, such as past exam papers and other practice papers (**see p. 85 for 11+ or p. 93 for 13+**). You need to show patience, perseverance and complete faith in your child. Most important of all, you need cooperation from your child. Nothing can be achieved without your child being willing to achieve it.

It is best to establish at least six months prior to the exams what preparation is needed. How much time you need depends on several things: the standards required by the school; the confidence you have in your child's present school; and, most critically, it depends on your

child. Pay attention to how quickly your child learns and how much they need to learn. A child who is bright but easily bored may benefit from an intensive revision schedule as exams approach, whereas a child who works slowly but steadily, and has a good work ethic, may prefer to start some time ahead with a gentler schedule (perhaps half an hour on school nights, plus an hour or two at weekends). Whenever you choose to start, the focus should be on the last six weeks or so leading up to the exams. Work up to that point in whichever way is best, so that your child is at their peak in the last few weeks. ▶

## Getting started

Before you start thinking about the specific subject areas your child needs to prepare, consider the two factors which will determine how well your child does in these exams: the length of their concentration span and the speed and accuracy with which they work. You can help your child with both of them.

Find out how long your child's exams will be and start acclimatising your child to sitting and concentrating for this length of time. Start practice early, with a relatively short period: a 20-minute practice paper, perhaps. Then, over the course of several months, gradually add to the work to be completed at one sitting. Keep at it until your child is comfortable concentrating on a specimen exam paper for the required time.

When you first start your exam preparation, you can afford to be relaxed about speed; the aim is to increase your child's familiarity with the subject and exam format. As the exams approach, however, your child should be working against the clock. In English, your child must write both

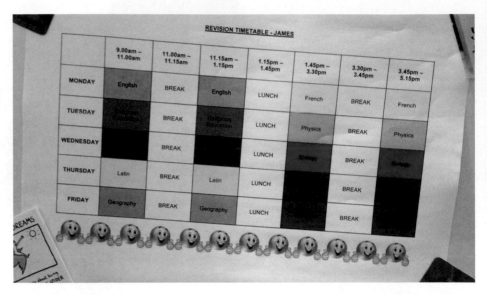

fast and legibly. In Maths and Reasoning, your child must be working with care and attention to the possibility of small mistakes. Slowly increase the number of questions at a sitting, until your child completes the specimen exam papers in the time available, with some minutes remaining for checking answers.

## Revision programmes

Many parents find it helpful to work out a preparation programme. Do not be influenced by what others are doing; your programme should target the areas where your child's attainment is weakest. If your child is weak in spelling or grammar, for example, find ten minutes each day to concentrate on them; if your child is to sit a Verbal Reasoning exam, it will take some time to become familiar with them. Focusing on their weaknesses may appear arduous to your child, so it will be helpful to work out ways of making it enjoyable—or at least, less taxing. Break the work into small and achievable chunks and reward your child when each chunk is achieved, and find interesting activities to include in the preparation programme for variety. Remember, a few minutes will be needed at the beginning of each session for going over mistakes from the previous session, and a few minutes at the end for reinforcing what has been learnt.

## Working together with the school

If you are helping your child prepare for these exams, tell your child's teacher that this is what you are doing and get his or her advice on how to go about it. Explain that you want to work with the teacher to achieve the best for your child. (Whatever you do, do not let the teacher feel that you are making up for any deficiencies on their part.) The teacher may offer suggestions about where to concentrate your energies and may even have materials and resources to send home with your child. The teacher should be positive about your contribution and pleased for your help. They should not put you off by telling you that it is unnecessary. If they do, trust your own judgement: the responsibility for your child's success lies with you. ∎

"We relied heavily on memory cards when my son was preparing for 13+ exams. We used them for everything: all the vocab and grammar in the languages, every date and name in History, every fact and definition in Geography and RS. So, when it came to revision, I'd just pick up a pile and start testing him. It's a very simple and effective method, and my son liked it because he could actually see the progress he was making, as the pile of cards became smaller. The greatest difficulty we found was that these revision sessions could be very soporific! So, with my second child, we added an element of physical activity to keep us alert: with each word card, we would throw a ball back and forth between us. This extra effort kept us awake and extended our revision sessions enormously. It also helped her ball skills ..."

ROSE, MOTHER OF 18-YEAR-OLD BOY AND 15-YEAR-OLD GIRL

"When my daughter first sat down to do the 11+ practice papers, she really was quite hopeless! She'd take a minute to sharpen her pencil; she'd look over the paper; she'd sit and ponder for a while... and at the end of half an hour, nothing had been done. But we soldiered on, and slowly things started to improve. By the time of the exams, we had it pretty well sorted. I was surprised; I honestly didn't think it would be possible at first."

CYNTHIA, MOTHER OF A LONDON DAY SCHOOL APPLICANT

Jupiterimages/CREATAS/THINKSTOCK

**AUTHOR'S TIPS**

# 7 WAYS TO **SUPPORT YOUR CHILD**

**1** Help make a good set of **exam preparation notes**. At this age, children still have trouble sorting out what is fundamental and what is mere detail, so it may be helpful to go through school notes together with your child.

**2** **Test your child** until they are absolutely confident about every name, place, date and definition. Remind your child that they need to know the lot.

**3** Help your child make up **vocabulary sheets** for languages.

**4** Make **small memory cards**. Do not buy these from a shop; half the learning is done when a child makes cards of their own. (It's easy: cut up sheets of plain A4 paper, write a word or event on one side and write its meaning or date on the other.) The cards make it easy to sort what has been learned from what has not, and to learn 'a little and often', which is the best way to learn.

**5** Help your child to **write clearly and concisely**: one point per paragraph. This is something that most children do not achieve until much later.

**6** Help your child to **prepare essays in outline**, so that they have an idea in advance what they could write if particular exam questions crop up. Ask your child to 'talk you through' essays from memory. Assume about six or eight paragraphs;

ask your child to tell you what each paragraph will contain. It saves time if your child can simply reel out a pre-prepared essay, leaving more time for the questions they have not anticipated.

**7** Obtain the ISEB **past papers** in each subject and go through them with your child. If this is not being done by your child's prep school, stage mock exams, using either the ISEB past exam papers or the exam papers set by the schools themselves.

anyaberkut/ISTOCK/THINKSTOCK

# SHOULD I HIRE A TUTOR?

**Looming over any discussion of exam preparation is this question: does my child need a tutor to succeed in these exams?**

cwzahner/iSTOCK/THINKSTOCK

The first point to make about exam preparation is this: it is probably not wise to rely entirely on your child's present school to prepare for these exams, no matter how good the school is. Some schools—even 'prep' schools—provide very little preparation at all. Other schools provide a great deal of preparation, but the specific form of preparation your child needs may not be included in the programme. (Perhaps there are other children in your child's class with more pressing needs.) Try to establish for yourself exactly what is being done and whether it is sufficient for your child. Identify where the gaps lie; merely getting your child

> Exact figures are hard to come by, but it is widely reported that in the cut-throat London environment, 50% or more of children are being tutored in the months prior to their 11+ and 13+ exams and pre-tests.

to articulate what they have trouble with will help them.

## How tutoring can help

In recent years, tutoring has become commonplace because entry for many schools is so competitive that children cannot afford to fall behind their tutored classmates. Many parents claim that tutoring has been hugely beneficial to their children, as it provides personalised help directed to the specific needs of the child. It occurs in the home environment, where a child feels comfortable and can express their difficulties more freely than at school. Tutors are often young undergraduates with a youthful enthusiasm for their subject—a perfect role model for a child. A tutor may inspire a child with enthusiasm for their subject where nothing else has.

Children who can most benefit from tutoring include: children with Special Educational Needs, for whom specialised and targeted tutoring is often advised from

an early age; children who are switching education systems or sectors, and must reorient themselves with the help of a tutor to a new curriculum; children who, through illness or mishap, have missed a stage of their education and can catch up with the help of a tutor; and children from underperforming

### HERE TO HELP

"Education of any type should be personalised to the individual learner to bring about the best results. Tutoring is a unique opportunity for a child to learn in a style which is engaging for them. Tutoring allows students to learn at their own pace, embedding subject learning at a deep level. This one-to-one attention and support allows children to develop as independent learners and build the confidence to achieve their potential in all aspects of their life."

**KATE SHAND, MANAGING DIRECTOR OF ENJOY EDUCATION**

Andrey Popov/PHOTOS.com/THINKSTOCK

schools. Tutoring can also be beneficial for bright but lazy boys, who lack the maturity of girls of the same age and might benefit from the added rigour a tutor will demand.

## The problems with tutoring

For the children already performing well at good schools, however, a tutor is neither a prerequisite to success nor any guarantee of it. It is better to work systematically on practice papers every day than cram for a tutor's visit once or twice a week. The academic levels required at 11+ or 13+ are not so high that the average parent cannot oversee a programme of exam preparation; checking answers, going over mistakes and setting targets is something that you can do together with your child.

Some Heads argue that if your child needs extensive tutoring to gain entry to a school, then you are aiming for the wrong school: your child is unlikely to be successful there, even if they are successful in gaining entry. Some Heads even express this view at their school's open day: 'If your child needs tutoring to get into this school, please do not apply.' Increasingly, the question is asked in

interviews: 'Have you had a tutor teaching you?' It is hard to know whether answering 'yes' will compromise your chances of admission, but answering 'no' will certainly not harm them (and lying is definitely not recommended— **see p. 80 for more on this.**)

see p. 80 for more on this.

The prep school Heads are also becoming increasingly vocal, because they see the day-to-day problems of excessive tutoring. Tutors' advice, they claim, sometimes contradicts the advice of teachers, resulting in confusion. Some children are being pushed to work longer and harder than is good for them; they then lose the downtime they need to return to their schoolwork with energy and enthusiasm. In turn, they lose enthusiasm for the entire admissions process—or worse, become antagonistic. Where children are pushed to attain levels of academic achievement higher than is natural to them, the result is merely that they flounder when they get to their senior schools. These children end up at the bottom of their senior school classes, where their loss of self-esteem cripples their chances of future success.

## Hiring the best tutor

If you do wish to hire a tutor, try to find someone who comes recommended. The market for private tutors is essentially unregulated and there is no way of checking a tutor's past performance, so keep an eye on

your child's progress. Your child's confidence and enthusiasm in their subject ought to improve fairly rapidly—along with their grades—otherwise there is no reason to keep the tutor on. Make sure that work is set to be completed outside tutorial sessions; a session once or twice a week is not actually enough. That said, be careful that your child is not overloaded with work. Your child's school homework must always take priority over the work set by the tutor. ∎

THE PARENT BRIEF

# Aiming High

Critical thinking skills to help my child excel at school

by Debra Price

**The Parent Brief's Aiming High teaches you and your child the critical thinking skills needed to ace any exam or interview**

# *We recommend...*

# KEYSTONE TUTORS

One tutoring agency we particularly recommend is Keystone Tutors. Keystone, founded in 2007, is one of the only tutoring companies to offer full-time salaried roles to professional tutors. This means you can guarantee that your child's tutor has been rigorously screened, and is known personally by the company, which has a tightly-knit team of 200 tutors. Many of Keystone's tutors are ex-teachers from top UK independent schools, and so are very familiar with exactly what your child needs to know.

The tutors work in and around London, but don't worry if you're based further afield: Keystone tutors can teach online to families based around the world.

Get in touch: 0207 602 5310
keystonetutors.com

**KEYSTONE TUTORS**

Will Orr-Ewing and Josh Pull, Founders of Keystone Tutors

---

# ENJOY EDUCATION

Another tutoring agency you can really trust is Enjoy Education, which was founded in 2006 by Kate Shand, and has gone on to win the Education Investor Award in 2013 and 2015, as well as being recommended in The Spear's 500 2016.

With Enjoy Education, tutoring can take place at home or online, and the company can even arrange to have a tutor join you on your holidays within the UK or abroad. They also have a Schools Advice team led by Vivienne Durham, who was the Headteacher of Francis Holland, Regent's Park for 12 years. Mrs Durham's expertise gives parents an invaluable insight into UK independent schools.

Get in touch: 0207 352 8800
enjoyeducation.co.uk

Kate Shand, MD and Founder of Enjoy Education

---

# FLEET TUTORS

One of the most established tutoring agencies is Fleet Tutors, who can draw on over 35 years of experience to provide an exceptional service to UK and international clients with children preparing for independent schools. They offer assessments, home and online tuition programmes as well as advisory services tailored to the needs of your child and your family.

Their network of consultants and tutors are well-qualified, fully vetted, understand the admissions process and have considerable success helping students through entrance exams and scholarships. A team of advisors work with you to choose the right tutor for your child.

Get in touch:
0845 644 5452
fleet-tutors.co.uk

Fleet Tutors
Helping students reach their potential

# WHAT ARE PRE-TESTS?

**Depending on which path your child is taking to admission, pre-tests may be more important than the exams themselves.**

Photo: Hawkesdown House School.
Photo: Eaton & Woods

Pre-tests are used by schools to filter down the number of applicants who will go on to sit their main entrance exams. They are commonly encountered before 13+ Common Entrance; children often have to sit pre-tests in Year 6 just to qualify to sit Common Entrance at 13+ for a particular school. However, pre-tests are becoming increasingly widespread before 11+ exams or 13+ school-set exams as well. Therefore it is important that you look into the procedures of the specific schools to which you will be applying, to determine whether your child will sit pre-tests.

Increasingly, the schools that conduct pre-testing are using computerised IQ tests, sometimes called Cognitive Ability Tests (or CAT tests). The tests require no recall of fact, so are held to give children the opportunity to show their underlying ability, rather than the quality of their schooling to date, and cover verbal, non-verbal, quantitative and spatial reasoning abilities. The tests are conducted on a computer, are multiple choice and are timed. As they are online, they can be conducted either at your child's current school or at the senior school.

Pre-tests work by standardising achievement across the range of values, according to age. The tests are adaptive, responding to the candidate's specific input across the range of tested fields, so as to develop a more accurate picture of the candidate's potential than standard pen-to-paper exams. The average mark in each of the tests is set at 100. The most selective independents will be wanting to see a result of 120 or higher in one or more sections of the test, since such marks correlate highly with A/A* grades at GCSE. (That said, ▶

## THIS MAY HELP

There is a very simple demonstration of the Common Pre-Test on the website of the test provider, GL Assessments, available via a link on the ISEB website.

## STRAIGHT FROM THE HORSE'S MOUTH

"When a boy has been accepted at 11, the school will, wherever possible, wish to 'pass' the candidate at 13+. However, a number are always turned away at this stage because, as sometimes happens, early potential simply has not been realised."

**STEPHEN ANDERSON,** FORMER SENIOR TUTOR AT WINCHESTER COLLEGE

Heads report that they have seen strong pupils perform poorly in CAT tests, so it is recognised that they are not fail-safe. Where they are used to assess senior school applicants, information from these tests will be weighed against other sources of information, such as the candidate's interview performance and prep school Head's reference.)

At 13+, the 'Common Pre-tests' set by ISEB are becoming increasingly popular. These are a form of CAT test, though the content is represented more conventionally as English, Maths, Verbal and Non-verbal Reasoning. The tests are extensive, lasting two and a half hours, and can be taken in one session or more. The benefit of these Common Pre-tests is that pupils can sit them in their own schools, all on the same day, thus limiting the disruption caused by pupils going off to different schools on different days to sit different pre-tests.

## Getting results

The results of the pre-testing may take weeks or even months to process—but you will receive them in plenty of time to register your child for the next round of exams.

Following pre-testing, a letter is sent by each school informing parents of one of three alternatives: their child has been pre-selected for a place at the school, conditional upon satisfactory results in the next round of exams; their child's name is on a waiting list for a conditional place; or the school will no longer pursue their application. In the vast majority of cases, the first category leads to admission to the school. The offer is conditional, but the pass mark is set at a level which it is believed the child is capable of attaining with a reasonable degree of commitment. Note that this mark may itself be understood in various ways: it may be an average mark; it may be an average, weighted in favour of certain subjects; or it may be a mark expected for each subject. If you are unclear about which is required, you should check; you do not want your child's results let down by a single weak subject.

The position of those in the third category is usually irreversible. However, you can always speak to the Head of your prep school and ask whether anything can be done; it is not unheard of for a child to move from the third category into the second. The situation

of those in the second category—the 'reserve' or 'B' list—is more nebulous than the other two. Schools usually will not tell you where your child sits on the waiting list. Some children will move into the first category over the course of the following months, their place being created by those who opt for another school. Some schools offer further pre-testing early in Year 8, after which further conditional offers are made. Lists will be substantially finalised early in Year 8, but there may still be movement after then.

For those on the reserve list, your Head may choose to make a phone call to promote your child on your behalf. There is anecdotal evidence that those who show the greatest interest in the school may be the most likely to receive an offer. Certainly, you should not badger a Registrar to express your enthusiasm or to ask for news: the Registrar will not feel inclined towards your child if they should feel harassed. You should nevertheless discuss with your Head whether a letter might be sent to the school if your child were to make excellent progress during their period on the waiting list, or become a prefect, for example. ∎

# WHAT ARE EXAM DAYS LIKE?

**There is a great deal of advice that you can give that will be useful to your child during the actual exam.**

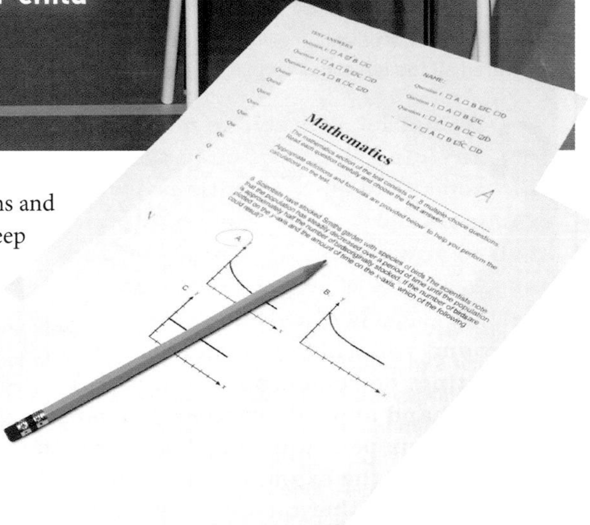

Fuse/THINKSTOCK

Give some thought to how you are going to organise yourselves on exam day. It's good to arrive about five minutes early—perfectly on time, but not so early that your child has to stand around amongst children who are all becoming increasingly nervous. Anxiety is catching. If your child is sitting the exam away from school, and has no-one they know to stand with, then stay with your child for as long as you can and keep them busy chatting.

Going into the exam, make sure your child has a bottle of water, spare pens and sharpened pencils and a watch to keep track of time. They may also like to bring a lucky charm.

The exam room may look intimidating, as it will probably look very different to your child's usual classes. The tables will be laid out in a grid, and not touching each other, so your child will be on a desk by themselves.

▶

has something to say about it. It may be best to let your child have the final say about what they take, because they must be happy to speak about it.

## Group interviews

Some schools interview in pairs or groups. These may seem especially challenging for a shy child, but do not assume that your child needs to be the most vocal in order to impress. The child who takes an interest in what is going on and then adds a pertinent comment at the right moment may appear more impressive than the child who tries to dominate the conversation. Your child should think in terms of what they can contribute to the other children in the group. The interviewer may ask: has anyone read a good book or been to a film they would like to recommend? Make sure your child has something to talk about. The interviewer will sometimes give the group a task, such as to try to describe a painting or make sense of what is going on in an obscure photograph. Your child's role in this situation is merely to help the group by adding a few sensible suggestions.

## How important is the interview?

Some schools value the interview highly; others rely more heavily on exam results—and they are unlikely to tell you where they place more weight. Furthermore, the interview's importance may depend on your child's exam results. At some schools, a child who performs brilliantly in the exams would have to mess up their interview badly to miss out on an offer, whereas a child whose exam results are lower than their peers (even if still good) will only receive an offer if their interview performance is exceptional. Since you will not know where your child is ranked, you cannot know how important the interview will be. You should therefore assume that the interview is important and prepare for it accordingly.

At highly selective schools, which distinguish themselves by their university admissions, the interviewer will be trying to identify the children who will get into the top universities. They will thus have these questions at the back of their mind: does this child have the spark that will grow in time to become something truly notable? Can I imagine myself and my colleagues putting in the extra effort this child needs to get a top grade? The school setting is about relationships, after all. The person who interviews your child will want to know that this is a child who will inspire—and deserve—the efforts of the teachers.

## Is it OK to lie?

The problem with lying in an interview is that it undermines your child's confidence. Children are not good at lying and, if the interviewer believes your child is dishonest about one thing, they may feel disinclined to believe anything else they have to say.

If you are planning to employ a tutor, you may wish to give this issue some thought. The school Heads are becoming increasingly opposed to tutors, and children are being asked at interview whether they have received tutoring. It is possible that any improvement in a child's marks that is attributable to a tutor will be cancelled out in the interview, either when the child admits to being tutored or lies about it unsuccessfully.

Another question which may provoke you to bend the truth is this: is this your first choice of school? Parents confronted with this question may respond that it is the favourite of one of the parents but not both, a favourite of the parents but not the child, or favoured for this or that reason but not for others. Or they may say, 'We are wary of making choices, for fear that our child may be disappointed. Each of the schools we have registered for is an excellent school and we would be thrilled to receive an offer from any of them.' A child confronted by this question may respond along similar lines: they can truthfully report that each school appears to be excellent, but that they like X and Y about this school and so would very much like to come to it. This is an excellent opportunity to teach your child tact. ∎

### THIS MAY HELP

There is a children's newspaper, called **First News**, which is intended for children aged 10–14.

# WHAT ELSE MIGHT THE PROCESS INVOLVE?

**Many schools conduct variations on the standard assessment process. So, to avoid surprises, find out in advance from the school what to expect.**

One variation on the interview is an activity session or day; your child may be asked to take part in normal school classes, for example. Boarding schools may ask children to come for a 'taster weekend' in which both the school and the child can ascertain whether they are likely to flourish in the boarding environment. These activity days may involve games, group activities of various kinds or even craft sessions. Your child should follow instructions carefully, participate with enthusiasm, and be polite, considerate and sociable. Your child does not need to assert themselves or show themselves to be a natural leader; they do not need to be particularly good at the activity itself. Enthusiasm and willingness to participate are what is important.

## The parents' interview

Many schools interview prospective parents as well as children—and many parents confess to being even more nervous than their children when they attend an interview. If you are interviewed, you may be asked about your home life, and how you support your child. You are likely to be asked about your aspirations for your child and how you believe your child will be served by this school. The best advice here is to be clear and articulate about what you believe the school can do for your child, and hence why you are so keen for your child to attend it. Point out the ways in which your child could profit from attending the school, but also what your child can contribute to the school—without bragging, of course. ∎

### STRAIGHT FROM THE HORSE'S MOUTH

"We try to choose girls who are all-rounders and will give things a go, so we tailor our interviews and activities to reflect this—and to give the girls the opportunity to show themselves at their best. We conduct a game in the gym, which gives the girls a chance to take the lead and be a little competitive; we also conduct a craft session to see how they concentrate on a task and follow instructions, and how they interact with and help others. If I were to give a single piece of advice to parents to pass on to their children, it would be this: be prepared to take part, to become involved in whatever activities are planned. Show some enthusiasm. You are not being tested in how well you can do the activity itself; you are simply being asked to join in, just as you will be when you come to the school itself."

**REGISTRAR OF A LONDON GIRLS' DAY SCHOOL**

# Parenting

Not all children are fazed by exams and interviews; some children enjoy them. For others, especially those with less experience, the admissions process may be nerve-wracking. Give some thought to how your child deals with stress. Many parents feel that the independent school admissions process puts an unnatural pressure on children to succeed. Even if you do not exert pressure on them, they may still feel it coming from others: teachers, friends, relatives, even themselves. You may thus find yourself desperately wanting your child to succeed but not wanting to add to the pressure.

Jupiterimages/PIXLAND/THINKSTOCK

## JUST BE THERE

Do your utmost to be there for your child during the exam period. Make sure that you have time together doing normal day-to-day things, so that your child has the opportunity to talk through any worries they may have.

## LIFT YOUR CHILD'S CONFIDENCE

Find specific reasons to be confident and repeat them. If you say, 'I'm sure you will do well', you are merely expressing your expectations and so adding to the pressure. If, by contrast, you say, 'Look at how well you just did in that practice paper', you show your child why they should be confident.

## ASK YOURSELF...

Is my child actually keen on the chosen school?

In interviews, particularly, a child's discontent may become obvious. There is no point applying to a school if the chance of being selected for it will be undermined by negativity at the interview.

## LOOK FOR SIGNS OF STRESS

Children respond to stress in different ways: some express it by becoming irritable or glum; others sublimate it. Look for signs that your child is flagging: some children experience sleepless nights leading up to exam day.

## ASK YOURSELF...

Would it matter if my child skipped this or that event and took the time to relax?

## GIVE YOUR CHILD CONTROL

- Take them to the bookshop to discuss which resources they would like to use.
- Let your child put together their revision programme and cross off the work as it is done. Some children will enjoy making charts and decorating them with stamps and stickers, or making spreadsheets and ticking off boxes.
- Give your child a say in deciding when they have done enough on a given topic and can move on.
- Have your child mark their own work. This will encourage them to take a critical perspective on their work and reflect on their strengths and weaknesses.

# WHAT WILL THE PAPERS LOOK LIKE?

While there may be variations from school to school, the papers do tend to follow a similar format.

CREATAS/THINKSTOCK

## English

The standard form of the English exam includes a comprehension piece (a short passage of fiction, non-fiction, or poetry, and some questions about it) and a piece of 'directed' writing (a short essay written in response to a prompt of some sort). Each of these pieces will be expected to take about 25–35 minutes, and are sometimes set as separate papers. Some exams contain further punctuation and grammar exercises.

In the comprehension piece, remember that every question asked relates to specific words in the text. The task is to point out the words which provide the answer, and elucidate, clearly and concisely, how this answer is given. As the exam goes on, the questions will increasingly relate to an implicit, rather than explicit, meaning. It is important that your child reads through every question at least twice, to make absolutely sure that they are clear about what the question is asking them to do. The greatest complaint of markers of English exams is that candidates fail to answer the questions asked.

A good trick to remember is that to gain one mark, you generally need to make one point. Where a point requires an explanation of an implicit meaning, this will often earn double marks, because it is more difficult. The marking scheme therefore provides a good guide to how much time needs to be allotted to each question: for example, if you have 60 minutes to gain a total of 100 marks, you have slightly over a minute to gain every two marks. Your child can use this to allocate their time appropriately.

In the piece of directed writing, the markers will be looking at the quality, rather than the quantity, of writing. Markers are looking for a good and original idea, presented in language that is varied and interesting. It matters less what the piece of writing is about than the atmosphere, tone or ideas it conveys. Good grammar and perfect punctuation are essential, and a sophisticated vocabulary will earn extra marks. The whole piece should be carefully structured, with dedicated introductory and concluding paragraphs.

## Maths

The standard form of the Mathematics exam consists of about 25–35 questions (some in several parts) to be answered in 45–75 minutes. Some will not pose a significant challenge to your child but others may be very challenging indeed. The most selective schools' exams venture into what may be described as mathematical or algebraic puzzles, which assume a certain mathematical ingenuity. These questions may be used by the school to identify potential scholarship candidates. Some of the more selective schools set two exams in Maths, the second of which will be much more difficult. (So a school may expect 90% in the first paper, but only 60% in the second.)

While there may be numerical problems at the beginning of the exam, the questions in independent school exams tend to be 'worded' questions: the mathematical problem will be explained in full sentences. The child will need to break down the question, paring away the verbal layer to get to the crux of the mathematical problem. The trickier questions ▶

# HOW WILL WE GET THE
# 13+ RESULTS?

Depending on which exams your child sits at 13+, you will have different sets of results to wait for.

Common Entrance children will receive two sets of results from the 13+ process: the results of the pre-tests and, some time later, those of the Common Entrance exams. The results of the pre-tests will typically be the more intensely awaited, since they will contain the conditional offer of a place at a school. Children who sit the school-set exams at 13+ will receive results from the schools in a procedure resembling 11+.

## Results of the Common Entrance exams

The Common Entrance results will arrive a week after the exams. Some prep schools organise a week of activities to tide the children through this period; if nothing is organised, find your own ways to keep your child busy and preoccupied. For the vast majority of these children, the outcome of the Common Entrance exams will be good news: the confirmation of the child's place. The school will not necessarily give the marks attained in these exams, but will usually give some indication of the child's performance as against other entrants. Any such grades will be specific to the school that awarded them; each school marks their Common Entrance papers by their own criteria.

For a very small number of parents, however, this will be a difficult time, if the marks their child receives in the Common Entrance exams are not deemed satisfactory by the preselected school. If this is your situation, the Head of your prep school will be able to guide you on your options. Your Common Entrance papers will be sent back to your prep school, which will send them on to other schools that may now offer a place to your child. The Head is in the best position to find such schools, by speaking to their Registrars; remember that it is in the best interests of your prep school to find a school that is appropriate for your child. In truth, however, this situation is rare.

## Results of the 13+ school-set exams

The results of school-set exams will be posted to you after the various testing procedures have been completed by the school. Some schools inform the prep school Head first, and then the parents. These results are usually posted

Wavebreakmedia Ltd/THINKSTOCK

fairly promptly after these exams take place, and should certainly be known in advance of March, when the decision must be made whether the child is to sit the Common Entrance exams for another school. By this stage in Year 8, parents will have had a great deal of time to reach a decision about which school they believe to be right for their child and should thus be in a position to respond promptly, should an offer be made. The only difficulty will concern those whose name is placed on a waiting list for their chosen school. The availability of places at the various schools

will become clear as the March deadline approaches at a preferred school. The parent is then in the unfortunate position of having to decide whether to pay a second deposit to secure this place at the preferred school. ∎

> "We were all watching out for that envelope; it was very tense as our son was applying to a very competitive and academic school. The CE results actually arrived in the post earlier than expected. We realised he had passed because the envelope was a thick one and we guessed it had the acceptance forms in it."
>
> **DEBRA**, WHOSE SON IS AT A SINGLE-SEX BOARDING SCHOOL

### HERE TO HELP

> "If your child has narrowly missed their required marks, then it's likely that the prep school Head and senior school Head or Admissions Officer will have a conversation. Sometimes this will result in the senior school accepting your child; it's not always successful, but the prep school Heads do give it a good go. If your child has missed their offer by a wider margin, then your child's CE papers will be sent to the second choice school. Your prep school can help by phoning your second choice, or indeed other schools. If this situation was likely, however, then your school will have advised you to apply to at least one back-up school—and it would be unwise to disregard this advice."
>
> **GOVERNOR OF A CO-ED PREP SCHOOL**

# Parenting

By age 13, your child may have sat many exams —but the 13+ admission process may still be worrisome, if only because it is so protracted: your child must first jump the hurdle of the pre-tests, and then sit the Common Entrance or other school-set exams themselves. The process may take a couple of years to complete.

fuchs-photography/ISTOCK/THINKSTOCK

## WHAT YOUR CHILD MAY BE WORRIED ABOUT

- It's reassuring that very few children fail their Common Entrance exams, but this may also feel like extra pressure to a child frightened of being the odd one out.
- The expectations placed on your child at 13+ often appear vague. Your child may feel unsettled not knowing the exact requirements of their chosen school.
- These exams are the culmination of two years of work, so it may feel like an overwhelming task.

## DEALING WITH COMPARISONS

After the results are in, your child may naturally compare themselves to their friends. Remind your child that different schools mark their candidates' papers according to their own criteria—and so your child mustn't feel bad about receiving a lower mark than a peer on the same paper; these grades are not strictly comparable.

## COPING WITH PRESSURE

13+ entrance exams are not far off the standard required in some subjects at GCSE. A child taking Common Entrance to a highly selective school, and requiring a set of results around the 65–70% level, is going through quite an ordeal. Understanding this, and helping them to cope, is quite a challenge for you too. Even for those applying to less academic schools, achieving 50% in such a wide range of subjects is putting a lot of pressure on them and you need to check that your child is coping. Help them to understand that their teachers have prepared them over the previous years, and nothing will crop up which they will be unable to deal with. Make them feel how proud you are of them. Just knowing that you are proud will help them through the last stages of revision and exam practice.

## AND ON THE BRIGHT SIDE...

In some ways, 13+ transfer is less stressful than transfer at 11+. If your child has taken and passed the pre-test, or if the school does not use pre-tests, then much of the uncertainty over the exam is removed. The school they sit the exam for has almost certainly decided to accept your child—which is not the case at 11+. So when the pile of revision notes and practice papers begins to get on top of you both, just remember—it's going to be all right!

## ASK YOURSELF...

Have you reassured your child that you understand what a lot they are coping with as they prepare for the exams?

# WHY CHANGE
## SCHOOLS AT SIXTH FORM?

Increasingly, the start of Sixth Form has become a time of transition within the independent sector.

Blundell's Sixth Form Common Room

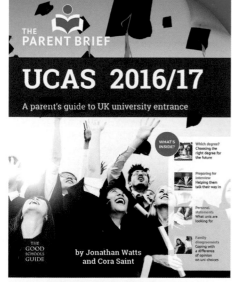

The Parent Brief's UCAS 2016/17 is filled with everything you need to know to get your child into the right university

Some children move because their schools do not have Sixth Forms; others, simply because they want a change. Moving schools after GCSE is an opportunity for a fresh start, a chance to revitalise a child's interest in school and in their studies. This is especially true of children who have attended the same school from their earliest years. Some girls move into some of the most prestigious boys' schools, which become co-educational at Sixth Form. Many pupils move from the state into the independent sector for their last two years of schooling, to capitalise on the lower staff:student ratios and the generally higher results of the independent schools. There is also some movement in the opposite direction, particularly into high-achieving Sixth Form Colleges, some of which compete with independents in their results.

Unless there is a desperate need for a change of school, the 16+ admissions process is typically less stressful than the 11+ or 13+, as children know that if they are not successful in their applications, they can always stay where they are. Many parents report that their children applied to one or two schools at 16+ merely to 'see what happened'.

## The importance of Sixth Form

Pupils who change schools at Sixth Form often do so because they are looking for a more stimulating academic environment. The Sixth Form is an important stage of education, in that it directly informs what comes after. Even more than at earlier stages, it is important that the academic level of the school match the aspirations of your child. Schools vary considerably in what they can offer pupils at this level—and these two years ▶

> "When you apply to enter Sixth Form, your child is also choosing their A level subjects, so it is a key moment in your child's life when you are advising them about their future. It is one of the most important decisions that will be made in your child's schooling, because the Sixth Form subjects determine what is available to them at university. If you've been in the same school since Reception, it's often a good idea to change for Sixth Form. It's an opportunity to look towards your future, to get excited about the prospect of becoming an adult."
>
> **DEIDRE**, WHOSE DAUGHTER MOVED TO A CO-EDUCATIONAL INDEPENDENT SENIOR SCHOOL AT 16+

of schooling must be approached with the confidence that your school can help you gain entry to the university or other higher education institution you're aiming for.

### Independence at Sixth Form

A change of schools at 16+ coincides with a general increase in what is expected of pupils at Sixth Form, in terms of self-organisation and self-discipline. The independent schools at the higher levels are usually very successful in fostering freedom on the one hand and responsibility on the other. Sixth Form pupils will be given a great deal of independence and will be expected to keep on top of their work and to engage in a range of other activities at the same time. In many schools, Sixth Formers can (within reason) wear what they like, come and go from school as they please, eat when and where they like and generally act much as they would if they were at university. At boarding school, they are given the facilities to cook their own meals—and indeed, this may be expected of them. If they are over 18, they may be allowed to go to the local pub on a Saturday night.

Sixth Form will be one of the most exciting times in your child's life, when the general broadening of horizons makes everything seem possible to them. Your child will certainly be required to work harder than ever before, but alongside this, many will also play harder than ever before as well. These are the years when your child will take the initiative in the organisation of their own studies and reap the benefits if their study habits are strong. But they are also the years when young people gain a new-found freedom—and some need help in working out how to manage their freedom to their own best advantage. ■

> "Moving was an excellent decision for my daughter. She has made many wonderful friendships, learnt to 'think on her feet' and gained a huge amount of self-confidence and independence. She has learnt to meet new challenges and embrace the new demands that were an inevitable part of making this change. She developed a real loyalty and commitment to her school and to her House early on. The Housemaster was extremely accessible, helpful and kind, always ready to resolve any worries and respond to any queries. The school made us welcome and we too felt a part of the school almost immediately. It has been a very positive experience for us all."
>
> **PIA**, WHOSE DAUGHTER MOVED FROM A LONDON GIRLS' DAY SCHOOL TO A CO-ED AT 16+

# The Sixth Form subjects determine what is available to them at university.

# WHAT IS THE PROCESS FOR 16+ ENTRY?

There are no standard procedures for entry at 16+, but there are certain things most schools will be looking for.

Madhouse/iSTOCK/THINKSTOCK

There are no Common Entrance exams for independent schools at 16+; in fact, many schools do not set exams at all. If your child does take exams, these will be conducted at the school, though provision may be made for students to sit them overseas. Any exams usually take place in the academic year preceding entry—that is, in Year 11. At the selective schools, those who are successful in the exams will be invited to interviews. Other schools may interview all applicants at the time of, or in place of, the exams. References will also be called from your child's current school. Because applicants will not have sat their GCSE exams prior to an offer being made, these offers may be conditional upon achieving the required results at GCSE.

## Entry requirements

Schools will typically state clearly the GCSE grades that are expected for entry at 16+: a certain number of A*s, As, Bs or Cs. (These requirements will be subject to change when the new numbering system for GCSE results is introduced.) Schools may also demand certain grades in specific subjects. Many schools require an A in proposed Sixth Form subjects, for example, though it is not difficult to find a good school that will be happy with Bs and Cs, if they come with a willingness to work at one's best. There is also a numbering system in operation in some schools: an A* being worth 8 points, an A worth 7, a B worth 6 and a C worth 5. The school will specify its requirements, somewhere between 50 (which corresponds to 10 passed subjects) and 80 (which corresponds to ten A*s). You may encounter other numbering systems as well.

It is important to ask the school whether the required GCSE grades that are specified are the actual grades that successful applicants are achieving, or merely the lowest acceptable for an application to be considered. At the most competitive schools, you may need to achieve higher than the stipulated grades if you are to win an offer against other top-scoring candidates.

## Entrance exams

The 16+ admissions exams are usually tailored specifically to the subjects your child intends to take at A level. Some schools require applicants to sit exams in each of the subjects proposed for A level study; others require applicants to choose some subset of these subjects—typically two—for examination. There are no specimen papers given out for these exams, but since applicants are working towards GCSE, these exams can be expected to be of a similar standard. However, the most selective schools will be looking for applicants who can show their understanding or develop their knowledge in original ways. Also, note that your child cannot necessarily expect the help of their current school to prepare for these exams: if your child is a good student, the school may not want to lose them.

16+ applications are made well in advance of the date when most pupils register their A level choices, so your child must have decided on their A level subjects in advance of others. Further to this, interviewers will ask your ▶

Monkeybusinessimages/iSTOCK/THINKSTOCK

your child about their intentions for university study, and their plans for making these intentions a reality. All in all, this means that your child needs to develop, by early in Year 11, a fairly strong sense of their academic future—no mean task! The answers that your child gives to these questions need not be definitive: there is of course the opportunity to change their mind during the course of Sixth Form. Nor does your child need to be set on a single course of action: they may quite reasonably report that they

are yet to decide between a couple of appealing alternatives. Your child should nevertheless be able to state clearly what the alternatives are and why they are appealing.

The 16+ exams pose a difficulty for applicants who propose to study subjects (such as Economics, Philosophy and Psychology) that are not widely offered prior to A levels. Applicants may not yet have studied these subjects in any depth and may not have a syllabus that is suitable

for revision purposes at this level. Your best approach here is to obtain the A level textbooks, and get a feel for the subject and the style of response that will be expected in these exams. Some 16+ applicants, however, choose not to list these as potential Sixth Form subjects; instead, they pick a subject where they believe they are most likely to perform well in the exam. Once they are accepted, the school will be unlikely to prohibit a change of subject in the months leading up to Sixth Form, when others in the school are still finalising their choices.

## Interviews

At some schools, applicants will be interviewed by the Head of Department in each of the subjects they propose to study; at others, applicants may be interviewed only once, by the Head or a senior member of staff. Either way, the interviews will be a particularly important aspect of 16+ entry: the schools will use them to establish what your child can bring to the school beyond their academic credentials. There will be an academic aspect to the interviews, but schools may also quiz you on other aspects of your CV. ∎

### HOW I FOUND...

## THE APPLICATION PROCESS

"The application process at 16+ was clear and straightforward. I had to sit written exams and, if successful in those, I'd be invited for interviews. It's hard to tell how competitive entry was, but the atmosphere didn't feel stressful in any way. I think only the school really knows what they were looking for. A good academic record was obviously a necessity, but they seemed to be looking for students who could think independently and who were excited about their subjects. Both in the written exams and at interview, there were questions about things I hadn't been taught before, and my job was to try to work out the answers using my thinking skills alone. Changing schools at 16+ was a brilliant transition from school towards preparation for university. I had to adjust to much longer days, travelling by train, rush hour, commuters and so on, and I gained lots of independence and self-reliance by making the change."

**Olivia, who moved from a girls' day to a co-ed day school at 16+**

# HOW COMPETITIVE
## IS 16+ ENTRY?

**Entry at 16+ can be fiercely competitive, but it is not necessarily the most academic candidates that will win places.**

The general rule for independent school admissions is that a selective school will become more selective the further you proceed up the school. Thus, the children at some of the most selective schools in this country, who have been through rigorous testing at 7+, and again at 13+, and then received the best schooling money can buy, may still find themselves being outshone by the newcomers who join their school at Sixth Form. As applications to the selective schools pour in from countries with exceptional standards (in the maths and the sciences, in particular) the levels of attainment of 16+ entrants become sky-high.

However, even taking the highly competitive London schools as an example, there are several factors that make 16+ entry more achievable than it might initially appear, even at the most selective of schools. Many schools increase their numbers at Sixth Form; a number of boys' schools create

places for girls in Sixth Form—and these girls then vacate their places at their former schools; some children leave the independent sector at Sixth Form, thus creating further vacancies. Even schools which are heavily oversubscribed at 11+ may have places available in Sixth Form.

What is more, even the most selective schools will not merely take the most academic of candidates. This would leave the current cohort of pupils dispirited: the new arrivals would simply outshine them. A school taking in new arrivals at Sixth Form will want to seed the newcomers across the breadth of subjects and classes, not have them stacked at the top. Schools will also want new pupils with a spread of broader interests, so that they populate the sports teams, the clubs and the various activities on offer across the school, rather than merely filling small pockets of it. Such schools will not merely take the applicants with the best academic

results; they will use the interviews to seek out special talents or interests that applicants can bring to the school.

Thus, while entrance at 16+ will be very competitive at some schools, it may not be selective in a way that can be anticipated. This should provide some encouragement to those wanting to apply to selective schools, even where their grades to date are not absolutely top-notch. ∎

Felsted, like many schools that offer both IB and A-Levels, has an international outlook

# SHOULD MY CHILD DO A LEVELS OR IB?

**Another reason students may change at Sixth Form is based on a decision to do either A levels or the IB.**

**A** levels are offered by almost every UK independent school and provide the standard qualification for entry to tertiary institutions across the UK; in this country, the A levels remain much better known to employers than any other qualification. However, a number of schools in the UK offer the International Baccalaureate (IB) Diploma to their pupils because they believe it offers a breadth and independence of study beyond that provided to A level students. What is more, some of the best-ranked IB schools in the world are in the UK. IB students are increasingly being accepted by the best universities in the UK

and worldwide. For international children, or children whose tertiary education may not lie in the UK, the IB Diploma may be a good alternative qualification. A further qualification, the Cambridge Pre-U, has also become increasingly favoured by the more

## THIS MAY HELP

The website of the International Baccalaureate Organisation (www.ibo.org) gives details of the IB Diploma and the schools that offer it.

Sevenoaks School offers an International Baccalaureate Diploma Programme. Photo Jonathan Cole

academic of schools, in part because of the confusion over changing A levels, but also because of the high quality and flexibility of the Pre-U courses themselves.

## The argument for the IB

The IB encourages critical thinking, discussion of ethics, independent research, and community service. IB students take more subjects than A level students, and across a more diverse range. While a typical Sixth Form pupil will take three or four subjects chosen from the entire range on offer, IB students take three compulsory modules and a further six subjects—and these must span a range of subject areas. This means IB students take on a greater workload than is common at A levels.

Sixth Formers walking in the grounds of Sevenoaks School. Photo Jonathan Cole

### HOW THE IB WORKS

• **IB students choose six subjects from at least five of the following groups: English, another language, a humanities subject, a science, a maths course and a creative arts subject.**

• **Students study three of their chosen subjects at a standard level and three at a higher level.**

• **The IB includes three compulsory core modules: a Theory of Knowledge module, which covers critical thinking and ethics; a 4000-word Extended Essay on a subject of personal academic interest; and the Creativity, Action and Service programme, which requires at least 50 hours in each of a creative, a sporting and a community service project.**

• **The IB is examined only at the end of the two-year programme.**

• **Each subject is graded from 1–7; UCAS values a 7 in a higher-level IB subject as the equivalent of an A\* at A level. Three additional points are available for the compulsory core modules, bringing the total possible points to 45.**

• **A pass is scored at 24 out of 45.**

The IB has a broader curriculum than A levels, making it attractive to those who do not yet know what they want to study at tertiary level.

There are only a handful of IB-only schools in the UK; most also offer A levels. Where both are offered, the decision between them can usually be put off until Year 11, when it will be influenced by your child's academic interests and intentions for university study. It is nevertheless worth being aware at an earlier stage that the alternative exists, since it may inform your choice of school. If you are considering an IB school for your child, find out the scores that children are achieving. The strongest IB schools will have pupils achieving a score of 40 or higher—a very good score. ∎

### STRAIGHT FROM THE HORSE'S MOUTH

"A third qualification is the Cambridge Pre-U, which is offered by some schools alongside one of the other two options. The Pre-U was once favoured by schools that didn't like the split between AS and A levels, but the recent A level reforms have made this distinction less relevant."

**CLAIRE OULTON,** FORMER HEADMISTRESS OF BENENDEN SCHOOL

"From my experience, the IB is the more difficult programme, not only in the sheer number of subjects the children take, but also in the level of the work. The level of the A level exam is not terribly high for clever children, as far as I can see, but the level of the IB is difficult for everyone. I think that the parents who opt for it do not want to see their children close as many doors on further study as you have to in A levels—but you pay for it in hard work. You have to be an all-rounder. One of the reasons I liked the programme was the Theory of Knowledge component, which I thought was excellent—lots of ethics and philosophy, and a focus on current affairs. It challenges the children's preconceptions and encourages open-mindedness. The IB is a premium qualification in the UK. If you want your child to do the IB, look carefully at the schools offering it and the scores they get. Scores at some school are stellar but others, I think, have trouble keeping up. My daughter did not have any trouble being admitted to Oxford with her IB qualifications. They are being accepted more and more by the elite universities."

**CATHERINE,** MOTHER OF AN IB DAUGHTER AND A LEVELS SON

At 16+, whether or not your child is transferring schools, they will usually have the chance to apply for a scholarship. Before making this decision, do consider the pressure that a scholarship application will place on your child. If they are staying at their current school, then they may find a failure to win a scholarship particularly upsetting; applying for a scholarship at a new school might add extra stress to the admissions process.

## Financial benefits

These days, the value of scholarships is not great; it's rare to find a scholarship that covers more than 10% of the fee, and indeed, many of the scholarships are purely honorary. However, at some schools, your child may need a scholarship in order to be considered for a bursary—so you may find that there is a financial incentive behind applying for a scholarship after all. **(See p. 12 for more details on the financial help available.)**

## Other benefits

Having a Sixth Form scholarship is a good way to make a UCAS application stand out when it comes to applying to universities. And it's not just the title that sounds good: at several schools, scholars also benefit from specialised programmes in their last two years of school, such as talks and seminars. ■

# SHOULD MY CHILD AIM FOR A
# SCHOLARSHIP?

**Scholarships at 16+ can bring financial and even academic benefits, but are they worth the pressure?**

Sevenoaks School
Sixth Form pupil.
Photo: Jonathan Cole

# Parenting

The majority of 16+ applicants are not applying to change schools because they have to or because their parents tell them to; they are applying because they want to. These children are old enough to know what they want from a school and what is required in the admissions process. There is nevertheless a great deal that a parent can do to help their child make this decision.

monkeybusinessimages/ISTOCK/THINKSTOCK

## ASK YOUR CHILD...

- What subjects will you take at Sixth Form? How many?
- What qualifications will you opt for: A levels, IB, Cambridge Pre-U?
- What will you do after school?
- What will you apply to study at university?
- Which universities will you apply to?
- What planning is required for your application: work experience, university open days and so on?

## REMIND YOURSELF

The decisions required at 16–18 may often appear overwhelming to those with little experience of decision-making. The need to make decisions about their future may come as a shock to those whose planning horizon had, until recently, extended only as far as their weekend.

## ASK YOURSELF...

How can I help my child learn how to make calm, considered and responsible decisions?

## ASK YOUR CHILD...

What will make you happy in the long term? Where would you like to be in five years ... and in ten years?

Then analyse their answer with them, and the steps between where they are now and where they would like to get to.

## IT'S YOUR CHILD'S LIFE, NOT YOURS

The decisions you make at 16+ must be based on your child's interests alone, not on your own wishes and aims for your child, on which you have based your decisions all these years previously. The question is not what you would do in their situation; the question is what they should do, given their specific interests and skills. Your task, in other words, is to try to look at the world from your child's perspective. If other parents' experience is anything to go by, you may find you very much like what you see!

## WHAT WILL THE ASSESSMENT BE LIKE?

There are no standard procedures for entry at 16+, but there are certain things most schools will be looking for.

123RF

At 16+, a school may assess each of your child's proposed Sixth Form subjects or some. An applicant is often expected to be strong in each subject, though a school may allow for a single weaker subject. Formal examinations are primarily designed to show potential for their subject, rather than knowledge of the GCSE curriculum. Candidates are often asked to take this knowledge, to reflect on it and apply it to new and unforeseen situations. Exams normally take place in the school itself. Some schools allow overseas candidates to conduct their exams at their present school, but many schools expect to interview applicants in person.

Some schools do not conduct formal academic exams at 16+ but rely solely on interviews conducted by members of the departments in the proposed subjects. The interviews will normally last about a half an hour. Candidates may simply need to talk about their interests, but may be required to perform a task and then discuss their work with the interviewer. The task is designed to allow a candidate to show flair and creativity of thought in the subject, rather than merely knowledge of their curriculum to date. A mathematics candidate might be asked how they would go about proving a tricky mathematical equation; a philosophy candidate might be asked how they would go about resolving a tricky ethical dilemma. You can expect questions that will challenge, so as to draw out the more able students. The best tactic is to outline your thinking as clearly and as succinctly as possible, showing your approach and the conclusions that follow from the approach you have taken.

Applicants at 16+ may also have a general interview by a senior staff member or the Head, in which they will be quizzed on their proven contributions to their present school, both curricular and co-curricular, and their proposed contributions to the prospective school. The interviews will in effect be a test of your child's maturity, teachability and interpersonal skills in general. Your child should be as polite, engaging and quietly confident as they can be, being careful to avoid appearing in any way self-satisfied or arrogant. Bear in mind in all the interviews that these same teachers will be conducting mock university interviews for the successful applicants two years later. This will be in the back of their minds as they interview 16+ applicants: is this child destined for success in their university applications? ∎

### STRAIGHT FROM THE HORSE'S MOUTH

"At 16+, schools usually look for a minimum number of predicted good grades at GCSE, but would almost always interview a candidate as well: the ideal applicant will show interest and academic potential in their chosen A level subjects or in doing the IB. Beyond this, schools also want to know that the student's social time at the school will be a success. New 16+ students need to settle in well to a school where friendship groups have often already been established, so schools look for applicants who are resilient and ready to join in."

**CLAIRE OULTON, FORMER HEADMISTRESS OF BENENDEN SCHOOL**

# HOW SHOULD MY CHILD PREPARE

## FOR 16+?

There is no standard way to prepare at this stage; your child will need to stand out to impress prospective schools.

No formal preparation is generally expected for 16+ assessment, beyond the preparation your child is already doing for their GCSE exams or their equivalent. The assessment at 16+ will normally be specific to an applicant's proposed subjects at Sixth Form. The best preparation for your child is thus to immerse themselves fully in these subjects, so that they are confident about why these are in fact their chosen fields of study and so that they have thoughts and interests to share with the interviewers from these departments.

In the months leading up to the 16+ assessment, your child should read widely in these subject areas. Their reading should extend beyond the topics on the curriculum, to show that they are committed to these subjects for their own sake and not merely for the sake of their exams. In the humanities, your child may benefit from an understanding of the history of their subject and knowledge of the major topics of contemporary debate within it. In the sciences, your child may benefit from knowledge of recent innovations in their subject and of areas of potential development in those branches of the subject that interest them. Your child should be aiming for a deeper understanding of these subjects and so might be helped by work experience or by talking to professionals working in these fields.

## Interviews

One difficulty your child may face in their 16+ applications is that they may have little experience of formal interviews. Their present schools will be unlikely to provide substantial help beyond the requested references, since they often do not wish to lose their students to another school at 16+. A parent can provide help by preparing practice interview questions and staging mock interviews. A family friend or relative, or someone less well-known to your child, may provide a more realistic interviewer. While it is difficult to anticipate the form that questions will take at 16+, both in exams and interviews, you might expect that questions will be less 'open' than at earlier levels. So, whereas candidates at the lower levels are asked questions amounting to 'Tell me about the book you are presently reading', an English Department interviewer may ask the 16+ candidate to contrast two books they have read in specific genres and to assess the relative effectiveness of the literary techniques used in each. In this way, the questions will require a basic knowledge of their subject, plus an ability to offer critical reflection on it. Likewise, in the sciences, candidates may be asked to push their subject knowledge at GCSE into new topics or disciplines. The candidate will be asked to manipulate their knowledge and apply it in unforeseen ways. Such skills can be developed ▶

THE PARENT BRIEF

## Aiming High

Critical thinking skills to help my child excel at school

WHAT'S INSIDE?

How to argue
Teach your child to argue convincingly in an exam
page 8

Current events
How to read the newspaper intelligently
page 24

Big decisions
Approach big decisions rationally
page 44

Exam tips
What the examiners want
page 104

THE GOOD SCHOOLS GUIDE

by Debra Price

The Parent Brief's Aiming High is full of practical techniques to lift your child's performance in exams and interviews

Students make use of Canford's calm and beautiful library to study

by sustained discussion around the topics in their chosen subjects, in the months leading up to the interviews.

## Branching out

Look for ways to demonstrate your child's broader interests and achievements beyond their activities at school. Those with sporting or artistic talents will of course be attractive to potential schools; however, your child's talents do not need to lie in the conventional areas. The independent senior schools, always keen to foster individuality and originality, may be particularly interested in your child if their talents lie elsewhere; they may be keen to set up an Amnesty Society (if the school does not already have one), a Feminist Society (of particular interest to the co-ed Sixth Forms), a Fendenkrais group (to calm exam-takers' nerves) or other such groups.

Give thought to how your child plans to support the various claims they will make about themselves in the interview. The interviewer will want to see a passion for the subjects that your child will study at A level, and it is wise to be able to show evidence of learning outside the syllabus. The interviewer will be interested in your child's plans for the future: what they want to study and what universities they intend to apply to. They will thus be particularly interested to hear about what they are doing to organise

### STRAIGHT FROM THE HORSE'S MOUTH

"There is one quality that I notice again and again in the girls who do well at my school and who then go on to do well at university: it is the tendency to ask questions. Asking good, searching questions shows that they have an inquiring mind, that they want to know more about what they are studying. It shows that they have a personal interest in the subject, that they feel that it affects them in some immediate way. This, I am sure, is why they do well. This attitude is evident in their writing; it motivates them to go deeper in their analysis than others who do not feel the same level of engagement with the subject."

**NICOLA,** TEACHER OF HISTORY AT A LONDON SELECTIVE GIRLS' SCHOOL

## AUTHOR'S TIPS

# A STRATEGY TO PASS ON TO YOUR CHILD

First, concentrate on your academic strengths and develop your individual interests. Your academic results to date are important, but the subject teachers who interview you will want to see evidence that you are not merely capable of good results, but are genuinely excited by your studies. Make sure you have looked through the A level prospectus and know what is involved in the A level courses in the subjects you intend to take. Read more widely in your chosen subjects, to broaden your interest and understanding, and familiarise yourself with the disciplinary approaches taken in these subjects. Find out what is involved at a higher level of studies again: the opportunities for university study and so on. Identify subjects that intrigue you— and read more widely on these. Think about how these interests might lead to further studies at university.

Second, make the most of your further interests and activities. Find ways to demonstrate that you have interests beyond the academic that will benefit the school. For example, if you have worked for a charity, consider how you might develop that work in Sixth Form and how it might contribute to a school programme of some sort. You do not need to have specific suggestions. The point is merely that the Sixth Forms in independent schools are very vibrant places. Study the school's website or prospectus and find out about the range of activities when you visit. Then, think about how you might contribute to making the school an exciting place to be.

work experience placements, to facilitate their university applications. The interviewer may also be looking for evidence of self-organisation and self-motivation, among other qualities. Your child should be prepared to be grilled on why they wish to change schools and what they plan to achieve once they arrive at the new school. They will be wanting to know that the inspiration to move schools comes from the child, rather than from the parents. ■

Sevenoaks School. Photo: Jonathan Cole

# HOW WILL WE GET THE
# 16+ RESULTS?

**Although you might hear from schools as early as December, your child will usually have to wait for their GCSE results to receive a formal offer.**

Many schools conduct their 16+ assessment in the November prior to the year of entry and so should make their offers by mid-December. Some schools conduct their assessments early in the year of entry and so should make their offers by the end of February. The dates for 16+ assessment will usually be listed on a school's website and the dates when results are posted will be given upon registration. Offers of a bursary or a scholarship will be made at the same time. As at other entry points, successful applicants have a short period in which to accept their offer and a deposit is required by way of confirmation of this acceptance. The deposit will often be a full or half-term's fees, an amount which may be deducted from either the first or the last term's invoice.

The school's offer may be unconditional but, for many schools, the offer will be conditional upon the applicant's receiving certain stipulated grades in their GCSE exams.

A formal offer from the school will follow upon confirmation of the applicant's achieving the required grades in their GCSE exams. If your child were not to meet their stipulated grades, you should contact the school promptly to discuss with them whether any provision can be made for your child. If there are extenuating circumstances of any kind, the school may be inclined to vary the terms of their offer. Some schools are known to be inflexible, however. If an applicant does not meet their conditional offer, your deposit will normally be refunded. ■

"Waiting for the results was a tense time, but thankfully we did not have long to wait. Our daughter took the exam in the autumn term of her GCSE year and it was only about three weeks later that we received the good news in a letter. This gave us great confidence that we had made the right decision for her future."

**MELINDA,** WHOSE DAUGHTER TRANSFERRED TO A CO-ED SIXTH FORM

# Parenting

The stress of 16+ admissions depends largely on the reasons for the proposed change of school and how badly your child wants the change. Some 16+ applicants come from schools with no Sixth Form; for them the necessity of finding a school may increase the pressure. Other 16+ applicants wish to change schools on academic or social grounds. They should feel less pressured because they have their present school to fall back on. However, there is an increasing tendency to change schools at 16+, with the result that children who in the past may have been perfectly content to remain where they are, now feel obliged to consider a move.

## REMIND YOURSELF

If your child has made this decision themselves, they may feel more personally invested than at earlier admissions stages—and so their disappointment if they do not succeed may be far greater.

## SORTING PRIORITIES

Remember, the most important thing your child needs to be doing at this stage is preparing for their GCSEs. If you are having trouble focusing their attention away from their Sixth Form application, remind them that any offer they receive will most likely be dependent on their GCSE grades.

## DINNER TABLE CONVERSATIONS

Admission interviews at this stage are less about rote-learning material, and more about demonstrating flair and interest in a wide range of topics. So one of the most helpful things you can do with your child is merely to engage them in discussion of the things they've learned, books they've read, places they've visited and so on.

## ASK YOUR CHILD

If you do not get into this new school, how do you plan to achieve your university or career goals another way?

Your child will probably find they have more options than they thought.

## MANAGING EXPECTATIONS

It can be very hard to predict your child's chances at 16+, as schools may be looking for very specific characteristics and skills. Your child therefore can't assume that intense academic preparation will guarantee them a place, even at a school where academic performance seems to be the top priority.

# WHAT ARE MY ALTERNATIVE OPTIONS?

**In the UK, parents may choose to educate their children by any suitable means, and there are many types of schooling to choose from.**

In different areas of the UK, education is compulsory for different ages. In Northern Ireland, children must be in school from the age of 4, but elsewhere in the UK compulsory schooling only starts at age 5. Across the UK, children must be in school until they are 16 years old; in England, school is compulsory all the way up to age 18.

Depending on where you live, a selection of schools in the various sectors will be available to you. Which should you choose? It depends on many factors: financial, social, ideological, geographical and the purely practical. The most important factor in the decision for many parents is the quality of schools available in their area; a second factor is of course the cost. Some parents send their children to independent schools from Nursery to Sixth Form. Many parents—including a growing number of middle-class parents who were themselves independently educated—are restricting their use of independent schools to certain carefully chosen years of their children's school careers.

## Comprehensives

So-called because they are not academically selective in their intake, many comprehensives may nevertheless give preference to students with an aptitude for that school's particular specialisation, for example sport, languages or technology. Some may also select on the basis of faith: many comprehensives are affiliated with the Church of England or Roman Catholic Churches. For these, church attendance for several years may be a prerequisite. Comprehensives vary widely in their standards and outcomes. Since intake is usually determined by catchment area, the intake of a comprehensive will naturally reflect the local demographic. There are many high-achieving comprehensives which are of good quality, but typically these tend to be heavily oversubscribed.

## Academies

Academies are state-maintained but independently-run schools that have been set up with the help of sponsors. A great number of UK schools have converted to academies in recent years. These schools have had an injection of funds and many have profited by the increased attention to outcomes that have resulted. While not substantially different from comprehensives, in that they are not selective, academies are given greater freedom in certain areas, such as the hiring of staff, the choice of curriculum, the allocation of budget and disciplinary issues.

Many of those that are performing most strongly are heavily oversubscribed.

## Free schools

Free schools are effectively part of the academy program, differing only in that they have been established from scratch by interested parents, teachers or educationalists. The majority of these schools were originally faith schools, but the program now includes bilingual schools, schools with a STEM subject (science, technology, engineering and maths) or other specialisation. The free schools program is expanding and results are as yet mixed. However, there are a number of free schools which are outperforming other local state schools. Again, these are heavily oversubscribed.

## Grammar schools

For bright children, the 164 grammar schools

### THIS MAY HELP

The Parent Brief's **Grammar School Entrance** is packed full of advice for getting your child into the right grammar school.

that still exist represent a very good option, as some are among the best performing schools in the country. Competition for places at these schools is generally extremely intense. Entry procedures and requirements vary significantly across the country. Generally registrations are due in the summer of the calendar year prior to entry and exams are held early in Year 6, so that parents of children who have passed can add the school(s) to their applications for school placements in October. The difficulty of gaining a place in a grammar school is primarily that there are so few of them. They are restricted to a few select counties and, even there, you may need to live within a catchment area to stand a chance of gaining entry—hence a 'house price premium' in these areas. Many children, having passed the 11+ grammar school admissions exams, are nevertheless turned away from their local grammar because of insufficient places. A few grammars take applicants from beyond their local area and some even offer boarding facilities.

## State boarding schools

There are 40 state boarding schools in the UK, where tuition is state-funded and parents merely pay for the costs of boarding, which may be less than £10,000 per annum for full boarding and less again for weekly boarding. Some schools do not offer a large number of boarding places and some are for boys only, but the majority are co-educational. Most are comprehensive secondary schools or academies, and several are grammar schools. A couple offer boarding at primary level. Many of these schools are of high quality and represent very good value.

## Specialist training schools

There are a handful of excellent specialist arts schools in the UK, supported by the government's Dance, Ballet and Music Scheme. These offer fully-funded places to exceptionally talented children and maintain high academic and exceptionally high artistic standards. Also, at the 44 choir schools across the UK, fully-funded places are available to choristers, who often go on to gain music scholarships at senior independent schools. Most specialist schools offer boarding facilities.

## Sixth Form colleges

There are over 90 Sixth Form colleges in England and Wales and more opening, including some sponsored by independent schools. They are typically large, co-educational day schools. They differ from secondary school Sixth Forms primarily in that they tend to concentrate on classes and qualifications, and offer fewer extra-curricular opportunities. Unlike comprehensives and academies, they may select pupils, holding exams in prospective A level subjects early in the calendar year. There are a number of high-flying Sixth Form colleges with Oxbridge admission rates rivalling those of many independent schools.

Yun Yulia/iSTOCK/THINKSTOCK

## Home schooling

Children are not required by law to attend school in this country. Home schooling is not widely practised in the UK, but it is within parents' rights. ■

# CAN WE PICK AND CHOOSE BETWEEN **STATE-FUNDED** AND **INDEPENDENT SCHOOLS?**

Yes, you can. Because the cost of independent schooling has been increasing so significantly relative to wages, it is now common for parents to send their children to independent schools for some part of their school career, rather than its entirety, as was once standard practice. The major points of transition between state and independent sectors are at age 11 (at the end of Year 6, after primary school ends) and at age 16 (at the end of Year 11, after GCSE). The most popular 'mix and match' options are these:

Parents who live in an area of grammar schools or other selective secondary schools often choose to educate their children in independent schools for their primary years, on the basis that their children will then be well-prepared for the selective school entrance exams at 11+.

Parents who live near good quality primary schools often choose to educate their children in these schools until the age of 11, whereupon these children sit exams for 11+ entry to independent schools—either to senior schools with 11+ entry or to prep schools which prepare their children for 13+ entry.

Another option for parents is to keep their child in state-funded education until the end of GCSE in Year 11 and make the move to an independent school at Sixth Form, so as to benefit from the higher A level results that the independent schools generally achieve.

Some parents move their child from an independent school to a state-funded Sixth Form for the last two years of their schooling. They may have a strong Sixth Form College in their neighbourhood.

# GLOSSARY

**Boarding school** - any school, independent or state, where pupils live residentially during the school term, by contrast with a day school, where children live off-site. Boarding may be offered on several different models: full boarding, where a child remains at the school throughout the school term; weekly boarding, where a pupil remains at the school during the week but returns home on the weekend; or flexi-boarding, where a more flexible arrangement is agreed between the school and parents.

**Bursary** - a reduction in school fees, usually awarded on the basis of financial need. Bursaries may cover these fees in their entirety or in part.

**Common Entrance** - a set of exams, offered by many prep schools in the independent school sector, which test children for entrance into UK independent schools at 11+ or at 13+. It was formerly offered only at 13+, so the term is used primarily for the 13+ exams and the programme of study leading up to them. The Common Entrance curriculum and exams are set by the Independent Schools Examination Board (ISEB).

**Day school** - any school where pupils attend the school during the day only, in contrast to a boarding school, where children reside in houses at or near the school. A school may be day, boarding or both.

**Department for Education (DfE)** - a department of the UK government responsible for education and protection of children up to the age of 19 in England. The Department has devolved counterparts in Scotland, Wales and Northern Ireland.

**Extra-curricular activities** - activities which take place outside the normal schedule of classes. These activities are designed to encourage non-academic skills of an artistic, creative, sporting or social nature. They are usually selected by pupils according to their own individual interests and abilities.

**Grammar school** - one of 164 selective state-funded schools in England and Northern Ireland. These schools by tradition have taught an academic curriculum to the most academically gifted pupils in the state sector. Admission is based either wholly or in part on results of an 11+ examination, which is highly competitive.

**Head** - the Headmaster or Headmistress of a school; the person appointed by the governing body to be in charge of a school.

**Independent school** - a school that does not receive funding from either national or local government authorities, but is funded primarily by the school fees of its pupils.

**ISC** - the Independent Schools Council a non-profit organisation that represents over 1,200 independent schools, with over 500,000 pupils. It is comprised of a number of independent school associations—including the Headmasters' and Headmistresses' Conference (HMC), the Independent Association of Prep Schools (IAPS), the Girls' School Association (GSA) and the Independent Schools Association (ISA)—whose aims and objectives it promotes.

**ISEB** - the Independent Schools Examinations Board sets curriculum and examinations for the Common Entrance examinations at 11+ and 13+. It is an independent board of prep school and senior school Heads.

**ISI** - the Independent Schools Inspectorate is an organisation responsible for the inspection of independent schools in England which are members of the organisations of the Independent Schools Council (ISC). Through an agreement with the Department for Education, it is empowered to carry out inspections and produce reports on each school, which are made available on their websites.

**Pre-test** - a test of some kind—often a CAT test, for example—which is used to assess eligibility to sit for further formal admissions tests for entry at any level into an independent school. Pre-tests are widespread for 13+ entry and are becoming increasingly common at 11+.

**Prep (Preparatory) school** - an independent school, traditionally educating children of ages 8-13 in preparation for entry into public schools (see below). Now the term is used more widely for schools educating children for entry to the independent senior schools. Many of these schools also offer a 'pre-prep' for children from age 3 or younger.

**Primary school** - a school which educates children in Years 1-6, by contrast with a 'secondary school', which educates children in Years 7-13. In the independent sector, primary schools are commonly referred to as 'prep' schools.

**Private school** - another name often used for an independent school.

**Public exams** - a series of exams that most students in the UK sit during the course of their secondary schooling. The most important of these are the GCSE (General Certificate of Secondary Education) at Year 11 and the A level (Advanced levels) at Year 13. These exams are administered by several examination boards - including AQA, Edexcel and OCR - which are responsible for setting and awarding secondary qualifications for UK students. See 'Secondary Qualifications in UK Schools', below.

**Public school** - a term used to refer to a sub-group of UK independent schools: the older, more exclusive of the schools, which traditionally educated boys of ages 13-18 in a boarding house setting. The term is now used more widely of schools whose Heads belong to the Headmasters' and Headmistresses' Conference (HMC). The term contrasts, not with 'private schools', as in some other countries, but rather with 'prep schools', which conduct the preparatory schooling.

**Secondary school** - a school which educates children in Years 7-13 of formal education in a UK, by contrast with a 'primary school', which educates children in Years 1-6. In the independent sector, secondary schools are commonly also referred to as 'senior' schools or 'public' schools (see above).

**Selective school** - any school—independent, grammar, comprehensive, academy or other—which selects pupils for entry on some basis other than geographical. Independent schools in this category are typically academically selective.

**Sixth Form** - a name commonly given to the two years of study (Years 12 and 13) in which students study towards their final school exams (AS and A-level, pre-U or IB) prior to entering the tertiary sector.

**State schools** (also known as 'maintained schools') are funded by taxes and are free to pupils between the ages of 3 and 18 years. State schools follow the National Curriculum and set National Curriculum Tests (NCTs), which used to be called SATs and are still referred to by that name. Over 90% of children in the UK attend state schools. Within this state sector are: comprehensive schools, which select children usually on the basis of the distance of their home from the school gate; grammar schools, which select children on the basis of performance at competitive 11+ exams; specialist schools, which specialise in certain subjects and select children on the basis of aptitude; faith schools, operated by religious organisations; academies and free schools, operated by educational charities; and state boarding schools, which charge for boarding (to a limit of £12,000) but not for tuition.

**Scholarship** - an award given to pupils, usually at the end of the admissions process, in recognition of academic, sporting, artistic, dramatic or other form of achievement. Most independent schools offer scholarships of one kind or another. Scholarships are often (but not always) attended by a reduction in school or other tuition fees, or may entitle one to be considered for a bursary.

# SECONDARY QUALIFICATIONS IN THE UK

**GCSE** - the General Certificate of Secondary Education is an academic qualification awarded in a specified subject. Students normally sit a series of GCSE subjects (in an independent school, usually 10-12) in Years 10 and 11 of their secondary schooling. They are examined in those subjects in Year 11 (though students may sit one or two exams earlier). Students pass with a grade ranging from A* to G. Many independent schools stipulate that students must attain a certain grade at GCSE to continue with that subject at A-levels. GCSE qualifications are administered by a number of different examinations boards, including AQA, Edexcel and OCR.

**IGCSE** - the International General Certificate of Secondary Education (IGCSE) is a variation on the GSCE academic qualification. IGCSE subjects are taught and examined in many independent schools, being considered more rigorous in some subjects than GCSE. Many independent schools 'mix and match' GCSE and IGCSE qualifications in various subjects. IGCSE qualifications are administered by Cambridge International Examinations. (See the Cambridge International Examinations website for more information.)

**A-level** - the 'Advanced' level qualifications are offered by most independent senior schools in England, Wales and Northern Ireland in Years 12 and 13 as the principal university entrance qualification. A-levels consists of two parts: AS levels and A2 levels. Students usually take three or four of each, involving a range of exams and other testing procedures, and are awarded a pass with a grade ranging from A* to E. UK and international universities standardly base their conditional admissions offers on a student's predicted A-level grades. A-level qualifications are administered by a number of different examinations boards, including AQA, Edexcel and OCR.

**Cambridge pre-U** - an alternative to the A-level qualification offered by a number of independent schools in some or all subjects taken by students in Years 12-13 and examined in Year 13. It is recognised as a university entrance qualification by top universities internationally. Students taking a full Pre-U Diploma are graded out of a possible 96 marks and receive a Pass, Merit or Distinction grade for each of three principle subjects, an Independent Research Project, and a Global Perspectives portfolio. Cambridge pre-U qualifications are administered by Cambridge International Examinations. (See the Cambridge International Examinations website for more information.)

**International Baccalaureate (IB)** - a diploma awarded by the International Baccalaureate Organisation (IBO), headquartered in Geneva. The IB is offered by many independent schools in the UK and abroad, and is recognised as a qualification for most universities, both in the UK and internationally. Students taking a full IB Diploma are graded out of a possible 45 marks, in six subjects (of which at least three are studied at a higher level), an extended essay, a 'Theory of Knowledge' programme and a 'Creativity, action, service' (CAS) programme. (See the IBO's website for more information.)

**Higher and Advanced Higher (Scotland)** - in the Scottish secondary education system, the Higher is the national school-leaving certificate exams of the Scottish Qualifications Certificate (SQC), equivalent to the AS in the English system. Advanced Higher is an optional further qualification, equivalent to A2, normally taken after students have completed Highers, for university entrance. These qualifications are administered by the Scottish Qualifications Authority (SQA).

# USEFUL WEBSITES

**Association for the Education and Guardianship of International Students (AEGIS):** aegisuk.net

**BBC Bitesize:** www.bbc.co.uk/bitesize/ks2

**Best Schools:** www.best-schools.co.uk

**Cambridge International Examinations:** www.cie.org.uk/programmes-and-qualifications

**The Council for the Registration of Schools Teaching Dyslexic Pupils (Crested):** www.crested.org.uk

**Department of Education Performance Tables:** www.education.gov.uk/schools/performance

**Eleven Plus Exams:** www.elevenplusexams.co.uk

**Galore Park:** www.galorepark.co.uk

**The Girls' Day School Trust (gdst):** http://m.gdst.net

**The Good Schools Guide:** www.goodschoolsguide.co.uk

**The Good Schools Guide International:** www.gsgi.co.uk

**The Government:** www.gov.uk

**The Headmasters' and Headmistresses' Conference (HMC):** www.hmc.org.uk

**Independent Parental Special Education Advice (IPSEA):** www.ipsea.org.uk

**The Independent Schools Council (ISC):** www.hmc.org.uk

**Independent Schools Examinations Board (ISEB):** www.iseb.co.uk

**The Independent Schools Inspectorate (ISI):** www.isi.net

**Independent Schools of the British Isles (ibsi):** www.isbi.com

**The Independent Schools Show:** www.schoolsshow.co.uk

**Independent Junction:** www.independentjunction.co.uk

**International Baccalaureate Organisation (IBO) website:** www.ibo.org

**IPSEA:** www.ipsea.org.uk

**The Mathematical Association Primary Mathematics Challenge:** www.m-a.org.uk/jsp/index.jsp?lnk=250

**The Metropolis UK Boarding Schools Guide:** www.metropolis.co.uk/business-publishing/uk-boarding-schools-guide

**Mumsnet:** www.Mumsnet.com

**Primary resources:** www.primaryresources.co.uk

**Russell Group:** http: www.russellgroup.ac.uk

**Scottish Council of Independent Schools:** http://www.scis.org.uk

**Scottish Mathematical Council Mathematical Challenge:** www.wpr3.co.uk/MC/

**The Spectator Guide to Independent Schools:** www.spectator.co.uk/the-spectator-and-education

**Tatler Schools Guide:** www.tatler.com/guides/schools-guide/2013

**UK Boarding Schools:** www.ukboardingschools.com

**UK Mathematics Trust Junior Challenge:** www.ukmt.org.uk/individual-competitions/junior-challenge

**Universities and Colleges Admission Service (UCAS):** www.ucas.com

**University of Cambridge NRICH:** nrich.maths.org/frontpage

# INDEX

# Other titles in The Parent Brief series

### Aiming High
**Critical thinking skills to help my child excel at school**
**Debra Price**

How can you help your child stand out and succeed in highly competitive environments?

Critical thinking is a skill that will boost their performance in interviews, exams and beyond—for the whole of their life. It's the difference between merely answering questions and really solving problems: an ability that will allow your child to shine and ultimately to maximise their potential.

- **Practical advice on how to encourage your child to think critically**
- **How to make decisions, argue convincingly and make the best impression on interviewers, exam boards and (later) employers**
- **Packed with insider information from the experts: interviewers at independent schools**
- **Checklists and real-life tips from parents who have already been through it**

ISBN 978-0-946095-2-8

### The UK Education System
**The essential guide to your child's education**
**Victoria Barker**

The UK education system is complex and confusing. What do you need to know to make the right decisions for your child's education from start to finish? This indispensable guide gives you straightforward explanations of the milestones and the options available at each stage, helping you to navigate your child's path through school with confidence and ease. From key stages to free schools, from sibling rules to home schooling, we shed light on the mysterious, cut through the red tape and give you honest advice in an easy-to-digest format.

- **Expert advice on choosing your child's educational path and getting the best from the system**
- **Inside information from teachers and heads across a broad range of UK schools**
- **Practical checklists and real-life tips from parents who have already been through it**

ISBN 978-0-946095-71-1

### UCAS 2016/17
**A parent's guide to UK university entrance**
**Jonathan Watts and Cora Saint**

Everything you need to know to help your nearly-grown-up child make a smooth transition from school to university. Not just a 'how to' on personal statements and application forms (although we cover that too), this book guides you through the process and gives you a clear understanding of the steps involved, the selection criteria and how to decide what's really important to your child.

- **The indispensable UCAS application guide to finding the right university and getting in**
- **From choosing a degree to applying for financial aid, writing a killer personal statement, surviving clearing and taking a gap year**
- **Inside information from some of the UK's leading universities**
- **Packed with practical checklists and real-life tips from parents who have already gone through the process themselves**

ISBN 978-0-946095-61-2

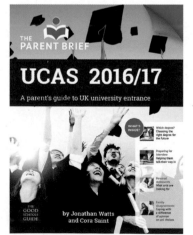

For more information and free advice visit **theparentbrief.com**